The Singapore Women's Charter

50 QUESTIONS

LEONG WAI KUM

ISEAS

INSTITUTE OF SOUTHEAST ASIAN STUDIES
Singapore

First published in Singapore in 2011 by
ISEAS Publishing
Institute of Southeast Asian Studies
30 Heng Mui Keng Terrace
Pasir Panjang
Singapore 119614

E-mail: publish@iseas.edu.sg
Website: <http://bookshop.iseas.edu.sg>

The responsibility for facts and opinions in this publication rests exclusively with the author and her interpretations do not necessarily reflect the views or the policy of the publisher or its supporters.

ISEAS Library Cataloguing-in-Publication Data

Leong, Wai Kum.
   The Singapore Women's Charter : 50 questions.
   1. Women's rights—Singapore.
   I. Title.
   HQ1236.5 S6L58   2011

ISBN 978-981-4311-07-6 (soft cover)
ISBN 978-981-4311-06-9 (hard cover)
ISBN 978-981-4311-08-3 (E-book PDF)

Typeset by Superskill Graphics Pte Ltd
Printed in Singapore by Photoplates Private Limited

CONTENTS

LIST OF QUESTIONS

FOREWORD

It gives me great honour to pen this message for a book on the Singapore Women's Charter. I remember living through those times before the Charter was promulgated.

The Charter was the end product of a series of events. There were many eminent individuals associated with its unfolding of whom many of us of my generation would recall the name of Mrs Shirin Fozdar. The efforts of many others should not be forgotten. To all of them, we should be thankful as the Charter represented a way forward for every woman in Singapore at that time.

Prior to the Charter, polygamy was rampant and battered spouses did not have any legal rights towards receiving protection. Undoubtedly the Charter changed much of that. The Charter also made it obligatory for a husband to maintain his wife and children during marriage and after divorce. By guaranteeing legal equality to both men and women in a marriage relationship, there was greater gender equality.

Many welcomed the Charter. But by no means did the Charter unturn gender inequality completely. If it did, there would be no reason for establishing AWARE (Association of Women for Action and Research) of which I was a founding member. For example, the Charter did not do enough to protect battered women and women whose husbands left them.

As such, the Charter was by no means perfect in its original form. In 1996, amendments were made to it — amendments critically needed to address gaps inherent in the legislation, especially to ensure greater protection to women and children.

But these amendments should not lead us to focus on the flaws of the Charter as it was crafted initially. On a more positive note, we should see the decision to amend the Charter as a reflection of society's increasing awareness of justice and equality as Singapore moves towards the 21st century.

From my own perspective as a woman activist, I am grateful for the Charter. It has brought on greater protection for women in the context of the family and, as such, greater gender equality in Singapore.

I am pleased that a book touching on this important legislation has been produced. While the effective and efficient implementation of the Charter is critical towards protecting the rights of women in marriage, a sound understanding of the Charter is also necessary. For every person who wishes to broaden his/her understanding of the Charter, this book goes a long way in achieving that goal.

Hedwig Anuar
Founder Member of AWARE,
Third President, AWARE (1989–91),
Women of the Year Award (1994)

PREFACE

The Women's Charter was enacted through a legislative process that began in 1960. It is, unique among family statutes, closely connected with Singaporeans' early stirrings of self-government and nation building. To commemorate the fiftieth anniversary of its enactment I am happy to attempt answers to the fifty questions that you might ask of the Women's Charter. In this effort I am greatly assisted by my colleagues, Debbie Ong Siew Ling and Chan Wing Cheong, who also collaborate closely with me in teaching Family Law at the Faculty of Law of the National University of Singapore.

Of the numerous statutes that apply in Singapore today it may be even more important for members of the public to become familiar with the Women's Charter. This statute regulates some of the most important events in our lives including marriage, and our relationships with our closest family members including our parents, spouse and children. As a Family Law academic I am aware of my duty to disseminate what little I know to assist members of the public in understanding this area of the law. In offering answers to these fifty questions I have tried to express the points as simply as possible while avoiding becoming inaccurate.

Beyond the technical content of legal rules that may be of interest only to legal practitioners, the law tells stories about us and holds lessons that we can learn. The Women's Charter tells stories about how we view family life and contains lessons of what we regard to be moral behaviour among family members. If each of us learns these lessons and behaves accordingly, together we build up our familial bonds so they remain strong. Telling stories about our common values in the hope that this encourages moral behaviour is another reason for this little book.

The law keeps changing. This book discusses it as of September 2010.

Leong Wai Kum
NUS Faculty of Law

I   WHAT IS THE WOMEN'S CHARTER?

1. What is the story behind the enactment of the Women's Charter?

Singapore Ordinance 18/1961

The Women's Charter was passed into law as Ordinance 18 of 1961 by the Legislative Assembly of the State of Singapore. The process of enactment began in March 1960. The State of Singapore preceded Singapore joining the Federation of Malaysia in 1963, and its becoming the fully independent Republic of Singapore on 9 August 1965 as it remains today.

General Elections 1959

The enactment of the Women's Charter was closely connected with the heady days of the political awakening of Singaporeans and their initial steps in the development of their own country. Singapore was a colony under the administration of the Government of Great Britain. Elections to only a proportion of the seats in the legislature were held in 1955 in the transitional process towards local self-government. The Labour Front offered the first experience of self-government when the first local chief minister, David Marshall, was installed in office. General Elections to fill a fully elected legislature were held in 1959. The People's Action Party, preparing to take part in these elections, promised in its election campaign to "*stand for equality ... of opportunity for education and employment for all Singapore citizens*".

PAP Five-year Plan

The People's Action Party announced a "Five-year plan" and identified, among other goals, its plan for the "emancipation of women" this way: *"Women who form nearly half of our population have an important role to play in our national construction. In the first instance ... a monogamous marriage law will be passed. ... Furthermore ... we shall carry out an extensive education campaign on family limitation and the rights of women. ... We shall foster the principle, if necessary by legislation, that there shall be equality of women with men in all spheres and we shall encourage them to come forward to play a leading role in politics, administration, business and industry, education and in other spheres."*

PAP's vision of marriage law

Elaborating on the marriage law, the People's Action Party announced that *"One of the aims of the PAP Government will be to introduce the necessary legislation to make monogamous marriages compulsory for all except Muslims whose religious beliefs permit polygamy."*

PAP victory

The People's Action Party won an overwhelming 43 out of the 51 seats in the Legislative Assembly at the General Elections of 1959 thereby wresting the right to govern the island. In June 1959 the People Action Party's Lee Kuan Yew was sworn in as the first prime minister of the State of

Singapore. From then on Singaporeans had full control over the development of their own country.

Women's Charter

In the First Session of the First Legislative Assembly of the State of Singapore in March 1960, the Minister for Labour and Law proposed the Women's Charter Bill to "*enact legislation which will make it an offence to contract other than monogamous marriages in future*". The proposal received near unanimous support including from Legislative Assembly members of the other political parties. The Women's Charter became the law on the formation of marriage and regulation of family members in Singapore on 15 September 1961.

Scope of application of statute

While the Women's Charter was enacted primarily with non-Muslim Singaporeans in mind, it was always a general statute. Today it stands as Chapter 353 of the 1997 Revised Edition of the Statutes of the Republic of Singapore.

As a general statute it applies to all Singaporeans except for the parts that are excluded from application to Singaporeans who married under Muslim law. The parts that are not specifically excluded apply to all Singaporeans. There are, therefore, parts of the Women's Charter that apply to Muslim Singaporeans as much as they do to non-Muslim Singaporeans. The scope of application of the Women's Charter in relation to non-Muslim and Muslim Singaporeans is discussed in Part IX below.

2. Why is this family law statute called the Women's Charter?

Long title

The long title to the Women's Charter still reads much as it did when it first came into force on 15 September 1961, that is, *"An Act to provide for monogamous marriages and for the solemnization and registration of such marriages; to amend and consolidate the law relating to divorce, the rights and duties of married persons, the protection of family, the maintenance of wives and children and the punishment of offences against women and girls; and to provide for matters incidental thereto."* This shows that the Women's Charter is a statute that brings together the law of the formation of monogamous marriages, the regulation of the relationship between husband and wife and the relationship between parents and their children, the termination of such marriages, and the regulation of economic matters among family members. It applies to men and women, as well as boys and girls in equal measure.

Raise legal status of women

The decision to call it the Women's Charter was explained by the Minister for Labour and Law when he introduced the proposed Women's Charter Bill in the Legislative Assembly in this way: *"This Bill is worthy of the description of being a Women's Charter. For the first time ... there will be monogamy in our community. ... There is no point in our talking about the rights of women and so on unless the*

woman is first regarded as the mistress in her own home."
Another minister added this insight: *"This piece of legislation
is only the beginning. But the more basic work ... is to
arouse the consciousness of women in our society, so that
they can more effectively stand up for their rights, and it is
only the women who can do so."*

Previous law unfair to married women

Both statements made during the debate in the Legislative
Assembly allude to the fact that before the Women's Charter
married women were less well protected under the law than
married men. One particularly grating legal concept under
the previous law was that, upon marriage, a man and the
woman came under the doctrine of "unity of personality".
Their legal personality became fused as one. Within this
fusion it was, unfortunately, the husband's legal personality
that was kept intact. The wife's legal personality was
subsumed under the husband's during the entire course of
their marriage. She became legally invisible and no longer
possessed the capacity to do things at law. Among other
legal effects, all the property she owned at the time of
marriage immediately became her husband's property as
she could no longer own or deal with property.

Women's Charter required to provide specifically for the legal capacity of married woman

It, therefore, was necessary for legislation such as the
Women's Charter to extricate the married woman's legal
personality from the "unity of personality" under the previous

law. The Women's Charter continues to contain provisions that list a married woman's capacity to do a variety of things. The fact that there is not a similar list of provisions of the married man's legal capacity should not be mistakenly read as the Women's Charter favouring the woman over the man, but simply that the married man's capacity was never affected by the previous marriage law in the way that the married woman's was. What was absolutely necessary to provide for the married woman was not necessary to provide for the married man. This is how the provisions of the Women's Charter which only speak of the legal capacity of the woman and not that of the man should be appreciated. What these provisions in the Women's Charter do is bring about an equal status under the law between a married man and a married woman. The existence of their marital relationship no longer makes the married woman lose her legal capacity. Neither husband nor wife is less legally capable than before their marriage.

Role in Singapore's economic growth

The Women's Charter was prominent in the process of Singaporeans' political awakening and played a significant role in their initial steps in national development. It reflects its first local government's wise foresight that the country would do well to nurture its girls as much as its boys and to encourage both men and women, single and married, to contribute to the country's economy to their fullest capability. Through all the contributions made by both men and women, Singapore has dramatically transformed its economy to become what it is today. The Women's Charter is unique among family statutes in having contributed to the country's development.

3. Should Singapore change the title of the Women's Charter now to the Family Law Act?

The good thing about changing the title to "Family Law Act" is that it will more accurately reflect the contents. The sad thing about doing this, however, is that Singaporeans may then forget what was traced above as the origins of this statute within the core aspirations of the nation's early local government. There is nothing quite as effective as retaining its intriguing title so future generations will continue to ask how it is that Singapore's family law came to be contained in a piece of legislation called by so grand a name as the "Women's Charter".

4. Where can a person gain access to relevant information regarding the family law in Singapore?

The Family Court website at <www.app.subcourts.gov.sg/family/index.aspx> is a good place to start. It lists a good deal of information on the laws that you will find most relevant, as well as how to go about making applications to the Family Court. It also tells you how you can contact and use community-based resources, including social services such as family counselling. The Court also runs very useful training courses including on aspects of parenting and how to develop better relationships with your family members. The website will even include some commentaries on the law and processes of court that you may find informative.

For more general information on the family services, you may also visit the website of the Ministry of Community Development, Youth and Sports at <www.mcys.com.sg>. If you wish to access social services immediately, you may select them from the "Marriage Central" website at <www.marriagecentral.sg/>.

II MARRIAGE

5. What does the Women's Charter require of two persons who want to marry each other?

Two sets of requirements

The Women's Charter makes two sets of requirements for those who wish to marry. One concerns the formalities of marrying, and the other relates to each party's capacity to marry the other.

The requirements of formalities refer to the minimum process the two persons must undergo in order to become married under the law. While the couple will usually also engage in other social functions with their family members and friends as part of their wedding, these additional social functions do not form part of the minimum legal formalities. The requirements relating to capacity to marry refer to the personal characteristics legally required of the couple so they possess full capacity to decide responsibly whether to enter into marriage.

Fulfilling both sets of requirements

It is only when a couple both fulfils the formalities as well as possesses the capacity to marry that the marriage is completely valid under the Women's Charter. Failing to comply with either requirement means a valid marriage will not result. Lawyers say that a valid marriage results only when two persons who possess the capacity to marry each other comply with the legal process of marriage.

Consequences of failure of compliance

Failing to comply with any requirement can lead to one or more of several legal consequences.

A most severe legal consequence follows the failure to comply with the most important of the formalities of marriage or any of the requirements of capacity to marry: the resulting marriage is completely invalid. Lawyers call such an invalid marriage by the somewhat contradictory term of "void marriage". Despite the contradiction within the term, it is useful in conveying the idea that, in fact, no marriage had ever taken place.

Then the Women's Charter identifies several causes of invalidity which, if they exist, allow the two parties to this "voidable marriage" to choose whether to apply to court to have their marriage annulled, or not to apply to court in which case their marriage continues as if it were a perfectly valid marriage. A voidable marriage may, at the parties' choice, either be made completely void, or it may continue as a completely valid marriage if they do not act to make it void.

The Women's Charter also provides a list of offences that may be committed by one or more persons in connection with the solemnization of marriage which fails to comply with its requirements. Indeed this list of offences is supplemented by the Penal Code (Chapter 224 of the 2008 Revised Edition of the Statutes of the Republic of Singapore) which provides for punishment of the fairly serious offence of "bigamy" that is committed when an already married man or woman attempts to marry another person in contravention of the Women's Charter requirement of monogamy.

Marriage law is serious

The point is that two persons who intend to marry are engaging in something that the law regards seriously. The Women's Charter specifies the legal requirements. All persons intending to marry must comply with them. Any failure of compliance can result in various consequences affecting the validity of the marriage and may even land either person in hot soup for having committed an offence. Frivolity should be shunned. Every person must regard the law of marriage responsibly and comply with the Women's Charter requirements with all due care. Question 10 below discusses how a criminal offence is committed when a couple attempts to use the marriage law dishonestly or with fraudulent intent.

6. What are the formalities of marriage in Singapore?

Process

The Women's Charter requires a process that begins with one person giving Notice of Marriage accompanied by a Statutory Declaration (*ie.,* a document of facts that the person swears to be true before a Commissioner for Oaths). The couple supplies personal facts that show they meet the legal requirements of capacity to marry each other, that they fully intend to commit to each other in marriage, the date they wish to become married, and the kind of ceremony they wish to undergo.

Choice of ceremony

The Women's Charter allows for a range of wedding ceremonies — a civil ceremony at the Registry of Marriages, a religious ceremony in a church or temple, or any other religious centre of the couple's choice, or a customary ceremony in any other building of the couple's choice, including the place they may hold their wedding dinner or the Botanic Gardens or Sentosa whether this be done indoors, outdoors or even under the sea. The choice is as wide as the couple wishes it to be. There is also a long list of persons, apart from the officials working in the Registry of Marriages, who are licensed to perform marriage ceremonies. The couple has a wide choice and could find someone from their religious affiliation or clan or community organization with whom they may be familiar to perform their wedding ceremony. The law permits wide choices so that the couple can make their wedding ceremony as meaningful as possible. The Registry of Marriages has also gone online so that people can communicate easily with it.

Public notice

The Notice of Marriage is put up for public information for twenty-one days before the next thing happens. The idea is to allow any member of the public who learns about the proposed marriage to provide any relevant information to the Registry of Marriages that might suggest that the proposed marriage should not be allowed to proceed. It is possible, if one of the two persons is already married to someone else, for this information to be made known to the Registry. Any information given is investigated and appropriate responses are then taken.

Marriage licence

After twenty-one days, if no adverse information comes to light, the Registry of Marriages issues a marriage licence authorising the couple to be married on their designated day of marriage in the manner they have earlier indicated they wish to marry, and by the licensed marriage official they have picked.

The wedding

At the wedding (at the time and place the couple has earlier specified on their marriage licence) the Women's Charter requires the licensed marriage official to ensure that the two persons fully agree to marry each other by requiring each to say solemnly that he or she is willing to marry the other, or similar words; that he or she tells the wedding couple the effect of being married to each other; and that there are at least two witnesses to the wedding. If either one or both parties are under the age of twenty-one, the Women's Charter requires him, her or them (as the case may be) to inform their parents and obtain their parents' consent to their marriage.

Signing

When the licensed marriage official determines that all the requirements of law have been met, he or she will invite the wedding couple to sign their marriage licence together with their witnesses, and then he or she will register the event as a marriage within the "Register of Marriages". The signed document becomes the married couple's Certificate of Marriage. The Certificate is good legal evidence of the couple having become married to each other on the stated day.

7. Who possesses full legal capacity to marry in Singapore?

Each person possesses the capacity to marry the other

Besides the minimal legal requirements of the process of marrying, the Women's Charter requires that the two persons intending to marry must possess the full capacity to marry. If any of the requirements of capacity to marry is not fulfilled, the two persons are not validly married, even if they comply fully with the legal requirements of the process of marrying.

Five requirements of personal capacity

The Women's Charter makes five requirements of the capacity to marry. One, neither person intending to marry is already married to someone else. Two, the persons must be a man and a woman respectively. Three, two Muslim persons cannot choose to marry under the Women's Charter (as they must marry under the Muslim marriage law) although one Muslim person can marry a non-Muslim person under the Women's Charter. Four, neither person is below the minimum age of eighteen years. Five, the two persons are not too closely related to each other as family members.

The basic idea behind these five requirements is simple enough and, except for the requirement relating to two Muslim persons that is unique to Singapore due to its separate marriage laws for non-Muslim and Muslim persons, the requirements are largely similar with requirements in most other countries. However, there is a good deal of background law to each of these which clarifies the rationale for each.

Waiver

The Women's Charter allows the fourth and fifth requirements to be waived by the Minister for Community Development, Youth and Sports if, on application to him, he decides that it is a fitting case for waiving the requirement(s) and allowing the particular marriage. Unless there is such a waiver, a marriage that does not meet these requirements is just as invalid as a marriage that does not meet the first three requirements. If waiver is given, the marriage is valid despite the fact that one or both parties is or are below the age of eighteen years or that they are related to each other in ways that would normally be regarded as too close for marriage.

8. Does the law allow a couple to incorporate additional religious or customary rites into their wedding?

The Women's Charter only sets out the minimum requirements of the process of marrying, and of who possesses the capacity to marry. It does not discourage a couple from incorporating any other rite, whether this comes from their religious beliefs or old customs that their families continue to practise, or even something the couple dreams up themselves, into their wedding. There is no reason for the law to discourage any additional rites that could make the occasion more memorable for a couple. Indeed by laying down only the minimum requirements of the formalities of marriage and allowing a wide choice even within these minimum requirements, the Women's Charter takes a modern approach to regulating the formation of marriage. Anything not unlawful can be added to a wedding ceremony celebrated under the Women's Charter.

9. How does the law of marriage apply to foreigners who wish to marry in Singapore?

Residence in Singapore

In terms of formalities, the Women's Charter requires that the two persons intending to marry should have resided in Singapore for at least fifteen days before they give Notice to Marry at the Registry of Marriages. Once they have lived here for this minimum period of time, a foreigner is able to use the process of marriage offered in the Women's Charter.

Personal capacity — Women's Charter and law of domicile

With respect to the requirements of capacity to marry, foreigners must still comply with the five requirements the Women's Charter sets for anyone who wishes to marry under it (discussed in Question 7 above). In addition, as foreigners are more closely connected with their own home laws (lawyers call this the law of their domicile) than with the Women's Charter, they must also comply with the requirements of capacity to marry under their own home laws, if these requirements are different from, or stricter than the requirements of the Women's Charter. This said, however, as the requirements of capacity to marry of the Women's Charter are fairly in line with the requirements of most other countries, it is not likely that there would be a case where two foreigners also have to meet the much stricter requirements under their own home laws.

No automatic waiver of Women's Charter requirements

Since the foreigners are seeking to marry under the Women's Charter in Singapore, they cannot argue that the requirements of capacity to marry are lighter in their own home laws so they should be absolved from meeting the Women's Charter requirements. The Women's Charter requirements apply to any person who wishes to marry under it and even the Minister for Community Development, Youth and Sports may only waive two of the five requirements, *viz.* that the parties are not too closely related to one another and the parties have reached the minimum age of eighteen years.

Only kind of marriage allowed under the Women's Charter

Some foreigners come from countries with laws that allow same sex marriage or same sex couples to form civil partnerships resembling marriage. The Women's Charter does not allow either. Two same sex foreigners cannot claim the right to marry under the Women's Charter just because their home law may allow this. They have to go home to do so. If they do so and then return to live in Singapore, it is not yet clear to what extent the status of marriage will be extended to them. The courts here have yet to be presented with such an issue. When they are, Singapore will have to begin to build up its law on the extent to which it recognizes a same sex marriage or civil partnership that has been formed under a marriage law that permits such marriage or civil partnership.

10. What is the punishment for using the marriage law dishonestly or fraudulently?

Two persons who give Notice to Marry under the Women's Charter have declared on a sworn document that they fully intend to commit to each other in marriage. If they proceed to perform their marriage ceremony as authorised by their marriage licence during which the licensed marriage official asks them to repeat that they are willing to marry each other, the law regards them to have fully committed to marriage. Supposing it is later proven that the two persons went through the whole process but never intended to become married and the woman say, only wanted to achieve residence status in Singapore as the "wife" of a Singaporean man, while the man received some payment for having assisted her, this could attract serious criminal punishment.

It is possible for a court to be satisfied that these two persons have subverted the marriage law under the Women's

Charter. The Penal Code (Chapter 224 of the 2008 Revised Edition of the Statutes of the Republic of Singapore) punishes anyone who subverts the marriage law by attempting to use it dishonestly, or with a fraudulent motive that excludes ever intending to become lawfully married. The court distinguishes between a couple who commits this offence from a couple in a completely innocuous and therefore different scenario where the two parties have become lawfully married but their marriage is unusually loveless or unsatisfying to the couple. Judges are trained to make distinctions of this kind.

11. What is the registration of a marriage and what does this achieve?

The law requires of the licensed marriage official that, once he or she completes the legal requirements of solemnizing the marriage, he or she should proceed immediately or as soon as possible to register the solemnization so there is a public record of every marriage performed in Singapore.

The registration is valuable for the couple because, on its completion, they receive the Certificate of Marriage. This certificate is good legal evidence that they are married and can be used any time they need to prove they are validly married persons.

The Certificate of Marriage is good evidence a couple is validly married until such time as it is proven otherwise. This means that, by itself, the Certificate of Marriage does not stop someone from proving in court that the couple is not validly married under the Women's Charter. After all, although a couple goes through the formalities of marriage, this does not result in a valid marriage unless both parties possess full capacity to marry each other. So, if this is not so, it can be proven in court and where it is so proven the court will rule that the couple is indeed not validly married under the Women's Charter. Where this drastic step is not taken, however, the Certificate of Marriage serves as good proof that the two parties are validly married to each other.

III REGULATION OF HUSBAND-WIFE RELATIONSHIP

12. What is the approach of the Women's Charter towards regulating the relationship between husband and wife?

The husband and wife are both at least eighteen years old going into the marriage. Most people marry later so the vast majority of husbands and wives, even at the point of their marriage, are already adults. The approach that the Women's Charter should and does take towards regulating their relationship is one of minimal intervention. The Women's Charter permits them to organize their lives together in any way that suits them.

The Women's Charter first sets out its expectations of the way a husband and wife will treat each other and steers them towards a reasonable view of what it means to be married to each other. This the statute achieves through the provision that provides a moral view of marriage as being an equal cooperative partnership of different efforts (discussed in Question 13 below). Then the Women's Charter fairly much leaves the husband and wife to their own devices.

The statute intervenes in their relationship only when it is absolutely necessary to do so. This is when either the husband or the wife falls so far short of what the law expects of him or her that it becomes necessary for the law to step in. Where violence is committed or threatened among family members (discussed in Part V below) is one clear instance. Where a husband fails to provide reasonable maintenance to his wife who is dependent on his financial support is another instance (discussed in Part VII below). The aim is thus as little intervention as possible. Only then can the continuing deep relationship between a husband

and wife grow stronger within the privacy that non-legal intervention provides a couple.

13. What does the equal cooperative partnership of different efforts mean?

Section 46(1)

The Women's Charter in section 46(1) provides that upon the solemnization of marriage a husband and wife are mutually bound to cooperate with each other in safeguarding the interests of the union. The provision continues to state that they shall have equal rights in the running of the matrimonial household, they shall have the right separately to engage in any trade or profession or social activities, and that a wife shall have the right to use her own surname and name if she chooses to. In short, marriage for the married couple means their equal cooperative partnership of different efforts for mutual benefit.

Different efforts

A husband and wife usually bring different skills into their marriage. As a result each of them will make different kinds of efforts during their marriage. The law does not differentiate between these efforts. The law does not favour one kind over the other; neither the kind that will bring money into the marriage nor the kind related to homemaking and childcaring. Both kinds of efforts are accorded equal value by the law for the simple reason that a successful marriage requires all efforts that both husband and wife make during their marriage. No marriage can continue for long if all necessary efforts are not made. Conversely, when all efforts are made, the law does not distinguish whether it was the husband or the wife who made the particular effort as there is no reason for it to do so.

The law leaves it completely up to a married couple to decide how best to divide the roles within marriage. Roles may be assumed according to the more traditional model (where the husband is the breadwinner and the wife is homemaker and childcarer) or it may be more modern or even quite iconoclastic. It makes no difference under the Women's Charter. All the statute seeks to do is to encourage a husband and wife into cooperating with each other in discharging all these roles because this cooperative and efficient distribution of roles provides hope for a long, successful marriage.

Marital partners

The Women's Charter regards a husband and wife to be partners. They are partners cooperating for their mutual benefit. The suggestion that marriage has some likeness to a commercial partnership is extremely helpful because when the marital partnership ends in divorce, any excess property or wealth left from the marital partnership should be divided between the former marital partners. This is discussed below under "division of matrimonial assets" (see Part VIII below).

Moral perspective

Through this view of marriage as an equal cooperative partnership of different efforts, the Women's Charter provides a moral perspective of marriage. The Women's Charter is not just a collection of legal rules regulating family members in their relationships with each other. Beneath the legal rules is discernible morality. If we learn to read the family law in Singapore with some wisdom we are able to distil the morality within it.

One clear moral thread runs through the Women's Charter provisions that regulate the relationship between husband and wife. Both are reminded that by entering into marriage each has committed to a cooperative partnership where, by joining hands and discharging different roles, they both work for their mutual benefit. The better they cooperate, the more they will both benefit.

Remarkable statutory provision

Section 46(1) describes marriage so many of the other provisions in the Women's Charter can be traced to the moral principle inherent in the provision. It is to the credit of the Legislative Assembly of the State of Singapore to have, in 1961, added this remarkable provision to its family law statute.

One exception

There remains one exception to the equal legal treatment of husband and wife. The law in Singapore inherited this aspect of unequal treatment from English Law and the Women's Charter continues this aspect although England and many other countries have long equalized their laws in this regard. As will be discussed in Question 37 below, only a capable husband can be ordered by court to provide reasonable maintenance to his dependent wife. In the reverse situation, as infrequent as it might be, where it is the wife who is capable and the husband who is dependent on her, the court is not empowered to make a similar order.

In all other regards, however, Singaporeans can note with some pride that a Women's Charter treats a husband and wife equally.

14. What does it mean that both husband and wife continue to possess autonomy in making decisions?

Decision-making power

The Women's Charter does not diminish the authority of husband and wife to make binding decisions as there is no reason for it to seek to make them any less able to decide for themselves. There is nothing to be gained from a law that diminishes the autonomy of a husband and wife so the Women's Charter does not do so.

In a well-known decision in 1993 the Court of Appeal in Singapore said that the law in Singapore does not tell spouses what to do or how to live their lives. The law leaves all decision-making within the marital relationship to the husband and wife. Only by the law respecting their autonomy is it more likely that better decisions are made and the husband and wife are completely happy to carry out what they have decided.

Non-interference

A husband and wife enter their marriage at maturity (since only persons who have reached the minimum age of eighteen possess the capacity to marry each other). The Women's Charter continues to respect their maturity throughout the whole course of their marriage. The spouses, as mature adults, are able to make decisions without outside or official interference.

Wide range

The autonomy of decision-making within marriage covers a whole gamut of decisions from the simple to the most profound. Thus a husband and wife can decide what they will eat for lunch, where they shall live, how often to visit their parents, what religion to continue practising or to adopt, whether to have a child, and how to bring up a child they may have. The Women's Charter respects any decision they make on all these matters and others. Marriage under the Women's Charter does not limit the life choices available to a husband and wife.

15. What does it mean that the Women's Charter encourages husband and wife to show reasonable consideration towards each other?

Section 46(1)

Section 46(1) of the Women's Charter reminds husband and wife that each should always show reasonable consideration towards the other. It does not specify in detail what this means as it would be impossible to attempt to specify this in the multifarious situations that present themselves during the course of a marriage. The stance of the Women's Charter is to gently but firmly nudge both husband and wife towards always choosing to behave with reasonable consideration towards the other.

Reasonable consideration

Reasonable consideration towards each other is the legal ideal. Any failure by either the husband or the wife to give reasonable consideration to the other spouse falls short of the legal expectation. The law, however, cannot punish each failure of reasonable consideration by either spouse as this would be overly intrusive. Frequent legal or official intrusions into their lives would do more harm than good.

Extreme failure

We can appreciate the stance of the law better when we examine what happens in the extreme case where one spouse fails abjectly to show reasonable consideration towards the other. When there has been an abject failure by either the husband or the wife to show reasonable consideration towards his or her spouse, the law regards the latter spouse to be entitled to use the proof of such abject failure as evidence of the irretrievable breakdown of their marriage so that the court may award this spouse a judgement of divorce that terminates their marriage (discussed in Question 30 below).

Legal approach

The approach of the Women's Charter may be summarized as follows. The Women's Charter lays down the ideal that husband and wife shall show reasonable consideration to his or her spouse. This expectation covers the whole gamut of their living together. Reasonable consideration means taking into account each one's likes or dislikes, and giving respect to each person's views and generally behaving reasonably well towards the other.

Any failure to do so is non-compliance with the law although the law will not intervene immediately in this non-compliance. It is only when the failures become extreme that there is response from the law. In the extreme situation where one spouse no longer accepts the abject failure of the spouse to live up to the ideals and applies to the Family Court for a judgement of divorce, the abject failure on the part of the spouse to show reasonable consideration will be taken into account by the Court. Where it is serious enough and where the safeguards within the law of divorce (discussed in Part VI below) are met, the abject failure can even result in the Family Court awarding a judgement of divorce that terminates the marriage. This is the optimal way in which the Women's Charter regulates the lives of husband and wife. The law respects a couple's privacy so it only steps in to intervene when the home situation has deteriorated beyond redemption.

16. Why is laying down the ideal, but not intervening until things are beyond redemption, the ideal shape of the law regulating spouses?

Minimal intervention

It is not possible for family law to regulate the relationship between husband and wife in minute detail. If the relationship is to have any chance to continue and strengthen over time the law must step back and respect a husband's and wife's need for privacy and space to develop their relationship. During the course of the marriage, the right stance of the family law is minimal intervention into the spouses' lives.

Social services

During the course of a functioning marriage it is better for social services to help the husband and wife when they encounter problems in their marriage. The law is not the only factor that shapes human conduct. Social services offered by community service centres, professionals or religious organizations are much more useful in helping spouses during the subsistence of their marriage. With some luck, a husband and wife who are experiencing difficulty in their marriage can find some assistance from these social services. If a husband or wife approaches the Family Court before his or her marriage is beyond redemption (*ie.*, when the marriage can still possibly be saved through counselling or by the spouses trying harder) the husband or wife will be referred to these social services. Useful links to some of these resources are available on the "Marriage Central" website at <www.marriagecentral.sg/>.

The Women's Charter contains a provision that reminds all personnel of the Family Court to remain alert to the possibility of reconciliation between a husband and wife. This provision is special because no one needs to apply for it to work — the Family Court officials are directed to keep the provision in mind! Where in the course of hearing any application, an official of the Family Court determines that the relationship of the husband and wife before him or her is not truly beyond being saved, the Women's Charter requires the official to stop judicial proceedings and send the parties for counselling to see if indeed they can be assisted by social services. Singaporeans are fortunate that in Singapore social services are easily within our reach. All we need is to be open-minded about seeking help and we will find that help is all around us.

Less acrimony

When social services have been exhausted and the marital relationship truly cannot be saved, it is then time for the law to come back into the picture. Here, since the marriage has irretrievably broken down, the aim of the law is to help a husband and wife end their marital relationship with as little acrimony as possible. The Women's Charter contains a provision that tells a husband and wife that, even as parties to a judicial proceeding in the Family Court, they are expected to be less acrimonious in court and that a modicum of reasonable consideration is expected to be accorded by two married persons towards each other in court.

Law cannot make us better people

Many of us may have come across cases where all this fails and a husband and wife who have been encouraged by the Women's Charter provisions to be cooperative during their marriage and to exhaust all social services before ending their marriage treat each other like enemies during divorce proceedings. Where this is unfortunately the case we need to realize that this is simply the weakness of the couple. The law is set down in the ideal way. The law cannot, unfortunately, make people better than they are. If people fail in their behaviour they only have themselves to blame. They will then be left to lick their own wounds. People who fail to treat their closest family members with as much reasonable consideration as they can muster will find that they create a lot more trouble for themselves than necessary. They put these relationships at risk and may lose them altogether.

IV REGULATION OF PARENT-CHILD RELATIONSHIP

17. How does the Women's Charter regulate the relationship between parents and their child?

Section 46(1)

The Women's Charter in section 46(1) directs the husband and wife that they are mutually bound to cooperate with each other in caring and providing for their children.

Parental responsibility

The Women's Charter tells all parents that they owe parental responsibility towards their child or children. Parental responsibility has become a commonly used concept since the United Nations-sponsored Convention on the Rights of the Child adopted it, but this international document did not exist until 1989. Singapore enacted section 46(1) in 1961. The concept has been a part of the law of Singapore for a good twenty-eight years before it became accepted by the international community as the moral way to convey the relationship between parents and their child! This is not to say that the United Nations copied the concept from Singapore but it affirms the moral quality of the family law in Singapore that some of the ideas within the Women's Charter predated their gaining international acceptance.

Assume responsibility

By becoming a parent a person assumes responsibility towards the child. An adult becomes a parent of a child either naturally through the biological process of conception (whether or not there was any medical assistance in the conception or gestation of the child) or through the judicial process of adoption. The details of the effect of assisted conception on parenthood are beyond the scope of this book. The point is that a parent assumes the role voluntarily. It is by no means forced on him or her. Particularly while a child remains young and dependent on the parent it is right of the law to view the parent as owing responsibility towards the child.

Cooperative

Parental responsibility is to be discharged cooperatively. The father and mother of a child are expected by law to cooperate with each other in caring and providing for him or her. Indeed, parenting may be said to require the highest cooperation by the parents as only then can the well-being of the child be assured. The law in Singapore demands no less of all adults who choose to become parents.

Moral perspective

The concept of parental responsibility conveys the parent-child relationship in a moral tone. In the old days, English Family Law used to convey the relationship as that of parents owning a series of rights over a child. Singapore had accepted this as her law as well.

From the enactment of the Women's Charter in 1961, however, the law in Singapore changed dramatically. From the law stating that parents own rights over their child, the law now states that parents owe responsibilities towards the child. English law has also made a similar change but the English Parliament took longer to do so — only with the enactment of the (UK) Children Act in 1989. It is a matter of some pride to Singaporeans that Singapore had acted earlier and expressed the moral view of the relationship between parents and their children. Parents in Asia are sometimes accused of being harsher on their children than parents in the West. It is good to know that the law in Singapore put in place the moral view of the parents' relationship with their children before many other countries did.

Intact after parents' divorce

Parental responsibility remains intact when the marital relationship between spouses is terminated by divorce. The Women's Charter clearly provides that divorce ends the marriage but this has no legal effect on the parents' relationship with their child. The parents continue to be expected by the Women's Charter section 46(1) to cooperate with each other to discharge their responsibilities to their child or children. If the former spouses feel any awkwardness about having to cooperate with each other they are expected by the law to get over this as soon as possible and to subordinate their personal feelings to the welfare of their child or children. The clearest illustration of this point is with regard to the legal duty, developed from the parents' responsibility, to provide financial support for their child or children. As will be discussed in Question 36 below, the Women's Charter provides expressly that the parents' duty of reasonable maintenance of their child or children remains exactly the same after they have become divorced.

Minimal intervention

Just as with the relationship between a husband and wife, the Women's Charter does not spell out in great detail what it means that a parent owes responsibility towards his or her child. The law expects a parent to do whatever is reasonable in order to discharge the responsibility he or she owes to his or her child or children. The Women's Charter only provides for a few detailed aspects. Naturally, a parent inflicting or threatening violence on a dependent child is punishable (discussed in Part V below). A parent should also make reasonable provision for the maintenance of a child and this includes providing a home for the child (discussed in Part VII below). What is reasonable will depend on many factors that may be relevant for consideration and this is discussed in greater detail in the Parts that follow below.

Responsibility extends to people hoping to become parents

The Women's Charter in its section 46(1) is expressed to refer only to "husband and wife". In a famous 1999 decision, however, the former Chief Justice suggested that the Court of Appeal regards the law as applying not only to parents but people hoping to become adoptive parents. This suggests very strongly that the better way to read section 46(1) is that parental responsibility is the proper way to convey not only the relationship between parents who are married but also parents who are not married as well as persons who are only hoping to become parents to a child. Parental responsibility is therefore the core idea running through the whole of the law in Singapore regulating the relationship between all parents and their children.

18. How do other statutes in Singapore affirm the idea of parental responsibility?

The core idea of parental responsibility is repeated in other statutes in Singapore. The Guardianship of Infants Act (Chapter 122 of the 1985 Revised Edition of the Statutes of the Republic of Singapore) in its section 3(1) directs all courts in Singapore that, whatever the actual kind of judicial proceedings, whenever an issue crops up relating to "custody or upbringing of an infant or the administration of any property belonging to or held in trust for an infant or the application of the income thereof", the court must "regard the welfare of the infant as the first and paramount consideration". This has been Singapore's law since 1965. What this direction means is that, even where the application before the court does not involve the child at all, if any issue arises which when resolved will affect the custody, upbringing, property, or money belonging to a child, the court must resolve the issue with the welfare of the child as the court's first and paramount consideration.

There can be no clearer affirmation of the centrality of the law's concern for the well-being of any child in Singapore. It stands to reason that, where any issue before any court has a bearing upon the child and his or her parents, the court must resolve it keeping the welfare of the child as its primary consideration. What is good for the parent must generally yield to what is good for the child.

Between the child and his or her parents, the parents owe responsibility towards the child and the courts always operate from this principle.

To cite just one other example, the Children and Young Persons Act (Chapter 38 of the 2001 Revised Edition of the Statutes of the Republic of Singapore) allows the authorities to remove a child temporarily from the care of his or her parents where the home environment is assessed to be severely disadvantageous to the welfare of the child. If the parents fail so abjectly in discharging their responsibility to their child as to create a home environment that poses some threat to the child, the authorities may assess it right to remove the child temporarily to a better environment in consideration of the welfare of the child. The parents must then improve and, on satisfying the authorities that they can better discharge their responsibility towards their child, they will be allowed to regain care of their child.

19. For how long do parents owe responsibility to their child?

The Women's Charter has several references to the age of a child. Beyond this age the child has matured into an adult. The parents of the adult no longer owe responsibility under the law towards their "child".

Child — for marriage

For the purposes of marriage, the Women's Charter provides that a child who has reached his or her eighteenth birthday possesses the capacity to marry although a child younger than that may obtain the approval of the Minister for Community Development, Youth and Sports to waive the requirement of the minimum age of marriage. Still on marriage, the Women's Charter then requires a person who is below twenty-one years old to obtain the consent of his or her parents to the intended marriage. The idea is that, although he or she is old enough to have the capacity to marry, it is wise for him or her to consult his or her parents. This is also an appropriate mark of respect for his or her parents from someone of such relative youth.

Child — for maintenance

For the purposes of the provision of reasonable maintenance, the Women's Charter directs a judge of the Family Court to issue a maintenance order to a parent to provide maintenance to his or her child that should not generally extend beyond the child reaching the age of twenty-one. Exceptionally, however, where there is a good reason to do so (*eg.* the child is physically or mentally disabled or the child is continuing to receive tertiary education) the court may order that the payment of maintenance from the parent to the child continue beyond the child reaching the age of twenty-one.

Child — for divorce proceedings

For the purposes of an application during matrimonial proceedings such as divorce, the Women's Charter provides that a child shall be understood as someone below the age of twenty-one.

Generally below 21 years

It may be said, therefore, that a child in Singapore is generally someone who is below the age of twenty-one years. Parental responsibility under law usually extends only to this age. For a good reason, however, a court may read the statutory provision on parental responsibility to extend beyond the child reaching twenty-one years. A parent owes responsibility towards his or her child at least until the child reaches twenty-one years but this can, for a good reason, extend beyond twenty-one years. This is the legal view. Apart from the law, of course, a parent may in some ways continue to feel some responsibility towards grown children. The point is that such feelings of responsibility are not legal obligations enforceable by the courts.

Growing child's wishes

That a parent owes responsibility towards his or her child at least up to the child reaching twenty-one years does not mean that the parent can ignore a growing child's wishes. A parent must always treat his or her child with reasonable consideration and discharge his or her duties in pursuit of the welfare of the child. If a parent were ever discovered by a court to be pursuing his parental duties for any other objective than achieving the welfare of the child (*eg.* if a parent did something "*just to show who is the parent around here!*") the judge will chastise the parent and, where this is appropriate, make an order or give a direction to the parent to pursue the welfare of the child as his or her first and paramount consideration.

Parent to yield to growing child's capability

It is now well accepted internationally that a parent should give due consideration to the wishes of a child and the ability of a growing child to make decisions for himself or herself. Where, in relation to a particular matter, a child may be under twenty-one years old but capable of understanding the matter well enough to decide for himself or herself, the parent is expected by the law to yield to the child's capability to decide. A parent should judiciously calibrate the exercise of his or her authority with the capability for decision-making by his or her growing child. As the child grows, a parent is expected to yield to the child. Parental responsibility means exactly as it reads and a parent is expected to do everything in his or her power to discharge his or her duties to the child in the best possible way to achieve the welfare of the child. The Women's Charter requires all this.

20. What does the Women's Charter being non-intrusive in a functioning family mean?

The relationship between the parents and the child or children is, just like the relationship between husband and wife, a delicate relationship that will continue for a long time. The correct legal stance towards such a relationship is to allow family members as much privacy as possible so that parents can discharge their responsibility towards their child or children out of the glare of a spotlight. It will do more harm than good for the law to shine a torchlight on the relationship continually.

In a well-known 1999 case the Court of Appeal in Singapore has settled that a court should aim to respond with all due speed where intervention is called for and, when it does intervene, to give only orders that are wise and would benefit the child. Judicial intervention into a relationship between parents and their child or children should, where necessary, occur with all due speed and, upon its conclusion, the court should aim to give an order that would help the child in furthering his or her welfare.

21. What does parental responsibility mean in custody applications in court?

Minimal intervention

A parent can usually discharge his or her parental responsibility outside of the glare of the law and the courts. In a functioning marriage there is usually very little reason to involve the courts in the parenting of a child.

Care and control, access, custody

When a marriage breaks down, however, and a former husband and wife live separately from each other some decisions have to be made regarding the parenting of their child. This is simply because the joint parenting that used to occur naturally by parents who are living together is now not as easily achieved, in practical terms. The law separates the exercise of parental authority over their child into three broad groups.

First is the daily care and control over a child. With which parent should the child live (with the corollary that this parent will make the small decisions a daily caregiver makes over the child)? Where parents cannot agree on this and bring this matter to court, the court must make an order on who should have daily "care and control" of the child.

Second, since one parent is given daily care and control, when should the other parent have "access" or contact with the child? An "access" order allows the parent who no longer has his or her child living with him or her some organized contact with the child. Third, is the residual decision-making authority (*ie.*, the authority to make decisions over major matters) such as whether the child should go to a local or international school or abroad to study or whether the child should undergo an elective medical treatment. The residual decision-making authority is referred to as the "custody" of the child.

No custody order or joint custody order

In a well-known 2005 decision the Court of Appeal in Singapore decided that, while orders regarding daily care and control and access must almost always be made when parents separate, it is not always necessary to make custody orders. If no custody order were made, this means that the courts are not changing what the Women's Charter in section 46(1) has directed *viz* both parents, although now living separately, are still expected to cooperatively discharge their parental responsibility to care for their child as best as they can manage in these circumstances.

The parent who has the child living with him or her must continue to cooperate with the other parent when it comes to making major decisions over their child. Preserving the direction to parents in the Women's Charter section 46(1) is ideal and the courts aim for this ideal. The parents may harbour grievances towards each other but the law continues to expect them to do their best. They should put aside as many of these grievances as possible and continue to try to cooperate in parenting their child.

Alternatively, if the courts decide to make a custody order, they will favour making a joint custody order. This order, just like the provision in the Women's Charter section 46(1), directs the parents to cooperate in jointly discharging their parental responsibilities towards their child. In particular, they must cooperate when it comes to the major decisions regarding their child.

V   VIOLENCE IN THE FAMILY

22. What are the legal protections available under the law in Singapore against violence that is inflicted or threatened by a member of one's family?

Criminal offence

Just as it is a criminal offence to use violence on a stranger, it is similarly a criminal offence to use violence on a member of one's family such as a spouse, parent or child. The offender can be reported to the police and charged with offences such as causing hurt, causing grievous hurt, assault, wrongful restraint, criminal intimidation, outrage of modesty, *etc*.

One exception to this general rule is that parents are allowed some leeway in the use of physical acts of discipline on their children. The law, however, only allows acts that are motivated by the parents' desire to instil discipline in the child. Parents who punish their child excessively or who are not motivated by a desire to teach their child, *ie*. parents who inflict violence as an outburst of their own anger towards the child, will have committed a criminal offence under the Penal Code (Chapter 224 of the 2008 Revised Edition of the Statutes of the Republic of Singapore) or the Children and Young Persons Act (Chapter 38 of the 2001 Revised Edition of the Statutes of the Republic of Singapore). An act of violence committed without the intention to correct the child is just as much a criminal offence as any other act of violence.

Inadequate response

The criminal justice system's response to acts of violence by one family member on another may not be sufficient for many reasons.

One shortcoming of the criminal justice response to family violence is that it does not achieve what the victim needs. This victim needs the violence to stop but not the offender (who has or used to have a loving relationship with the victim) to be fined or jailed. The normal criminal sanction may in fact have negative repercussions on the family if the offender is the sole or main breadwinner in the family.

Furthermore, a fine or an imprisonment term does not focus on the root causes that led the offender to inflict violence on the family member. The criminal sanctions punish one act of violence but do not directly help the offender learn to control his poor behaviour towards his family members.

Criminal offences also require a high standard of proof in criminal prosecutions. The family member, as victim, may not be able to help the prosecutor meet the criminal standard of proof since the acts of violence usually occur in private where there are no witnesses.

It is partly to meet all these shortcomings that an alternative approach is provided for in the Women's Charter for victims of family violence to apply for a "protection order" (discussed in Question 23 below).

23. What are protection orders?

Protection orders

Protection orders are orders made by the Family Court

which restrain the perpetrator from using "family violence" against a "family member". Unlike a conviction following criminal prosecution, a protection order may be obtained by showing on a "balance of probabilities" that such an order is necessary to protect the family member. Conviction following a criminal prosecution requires proof "beyond a reasonable doubt" that the person committed the crime he is accused of.

Application

The part of the Women's Charter on protection orders applies to every person in Singapore whether a Singaporean or foreigner and, if Singaporean, whether Muslim or non-Muslim. The law in Singapore protects everyone from family violence.

Family violence

The following forms of behaviour are defined by the Women's Charter as "family violence": causing hurt, wrongful confinement or restraint, and continual harassment with intent to cause anguish. The last type of behaviour encompasses verbal abuse and psychological/emotional abuse. Only force that is used in self-defence or by way of correction of a child under twenty-one years old is specifically excluded from the definition of "family violence".

Family member

Only persons who are "family members" of the perpetrator can apply for a protection order against him or her. The term is defined in the Women's Charter to mean:

(a)   a spouse or former spouse;
(b)   a child (including an adopted child and a stepchild);
(c)   a father or mother;
(d)   a father-in-law or mother-in-law;
(e)   a brother or sister; or
(f)   any other relative or an incapacitated person who in the opinion of the court should, in the circumstances, be regarded as a member of the family.

Persons who live together but are not and have never been in a legal relationship, *eg.* cohabitees, flatmates and domestic helpers, are not included in the list.

Advantages

There are three main advantages in getting a protection order over seeking criminal prosecution.

First, a protection order may be obtained on proof that family violence "is likely to be committed" provided it is necessary for the victim's protection. The victim has neither to wait for the violence to occur nor for it to be imminent before seeking help.

Secondly, a protection order restrains the perpetrator from using family violence and, in that way, prevents future acts of family violence from being committed. Criminal penalties, in contrast, only punish a person for what he or she has done but does not actively try to prevent the violence from occurring again.

Thirdly, the Family Court may grant additional orders if justified by the circumstances of the case. These can include ordering the perpetrator to leave the residence (termed an "exclusion order") and sending the perpetrator, the victim or their children to attend mandatory counselling sessions. This way the whole family can learn from this unhappy episode, move on, and perhaps become stronger for it. The objective is certainly worth aiming for.

24. How does a person apply for a protection order?

Magistrate's complaint

A person who wishes to apply for a protection order (called the "complainant") appears before a district judge or a magistrate at the Family Court to make a "Magistrate's Complaint". The complainant has to fill out an application form and first see a counsellor. The counsellor will assess the case and advise the complainant on the court process and safety measures that can be taken. The complainant then swears or affirms before a judge that the matters he or she stated in the application are true. If the application is in order, a summons will be issued by the judge. This summons orders the perpetrator to attend court and answer the complaint that has been made against him or her. The fee for issuance of the summons is one Singapore dollar.

Assistance in application

For those who may be physically unable to go to the Family Court to apply for a protection order or who may be too fearful to do so it is possible for the application to be made at an agency with a video link to the Family Court for this purpose. At the present time, this is only available at the

Centre for Promoting Alternatives to Violence (PAVe), TRANS Centre and the Syariah Court. Trained counsellors are on hand to help in the application process at these places.

Children under twenty-one years old and incapacitated persons (due to physical or mental disability, ill-health, or old age) may be assisted by others in making an application for a protection order. The application may be made on their behalf by a guardian, relative, person responsible for the care of the child or incapacitated person, or by a person appointed by the Minister for Community Development, Youth and Sports (such as executive directors of certain social agencies).

Notice to perpetrator

An appointment will be made for the summons to be served on the perpetrator (called the "respondent" now that the court case has officially begun). This gives the respondent notice that a court case has been started against him or her and he or she should prepare to answer it, if this is his or her wish.

Judge to give directions

At the first hearing of the summons, a judge will consider whether the parties should be referred for counselling, and will also give directions on how the case should proceed. Both the complainant and respondent must appear in court on the day of this first hearing. If the respondent is absent, a warrant of arrest may be issued to bring him to court physically. The aim of referring the parties to a counsellor at this stage is to assess the need for a protection order to be issued, to help the respondent take responsibility for the use of violence, to seek alternatives, and to take appropriate measures to ensure the safety of the complainant from the respondent.

Full hearing

If the respondent refuses to admit to the allegations of family violence and refuses to consent to a protection order being issued, each party will then have to give evidence in court to prove what he or she claims to be the truth. Witnesses may be called by either of them. After hearing both parties, the court will decide whether or not to grant a protection order and, if so, whether to include an additional exclusion order or counselling order as well.

Expedited order

If there is an imminent danger of family violence being committed, an "expedited" protection order may be issued on the same day once the Magistrate's Complaint is made. The order takes effect when it is served on the respondent or on a date specified by the court. There is no need to wait for the hearing of the summons. However, an expedited order is valid for only twenty-eight days or up to the commencement of the court hearing of the application for a protection order, whichever is earlier.

25. What is the punishment for breach of a protection order?

The law views the breach of a protection order with gravity. A person who wilfully contravenes a protection order, an expedited order, or an exclusion order commits a grave criminal offence. For such a breach, the perpetrator/respondent may be arrested by the police without a warrant of arrest. On first conviction, the person is liable to a maximum fine of $2,000, or maximum imprisonment of six months, or both. In the case of a second or subsequent conviction, the penalty is a maximum fine of $5,000 or maximum imprisonment of twelve months, or both. The sentencing guideline developed by the courts is that breach of such orders by the further use of physical violence will result in an imprisonment sentence even though the law gives the court discretion to impose only a fine. A fine is deemed appropriate only in cases where there is little or no physical violence in the breach, such as when the perpetrator/respondent only repeatedly harasses the family member after an application for the protection order was made by the family member.

A failure to comply with a counselling order made by the court is considered as contempt of court and is punishable as such.

26. What are the community resources available when there is a threat of violence from a family member?

An important resource are the Family Service Centres located all over Singapore. Counselling and support services are offered by trained social workers to those affected by family violence. In particular, two agencies which specialize in family violence work are PAVe and TRANS Centre.

For perpetrators with gambling and/or alcohol addiction problems, intervention is provided by counsellors at the Institute of Mental Health.

Children who are victims of family violence or have witnessed it may turn to an interactive website developed by the Family Court at <http://kidsnet.subcourts.gov.sg>. It aims to help children explore issues relating to divorce and family violence and give them information on how to get help. Parents who need assistance in parenting may turn to courses run by various social agencies such as the Singapore Children's Society. The resources give substance to the legal idea of parents owing responsibility towards their children (discussed in Question 17 above).

It takes a community effort to stem the scourge of family violence. Good coordination between the various agencies such as the police, the Family and Juvenile Courts, schools, hospitals, and social service agencies, is needed in order to ensure timely detection and effective intervention for both the victims and perpetrators of family violence. To this end, the Ministry of Community Development, Youth and Sports issued a manual with the self-explanatory title of "Integrated Management of Family Violence Cases in Singapore" in 1999 and updated this in 2009.

VI DIVORCE AND THE PROCESS

27. When can a husband or wife seek divorce?

The right way for any person to view divorce is that it offers relief where nothing else works. The law accordingly offers divorce as relief to unhappily married persons but this relief is rightly available only as the last resort after community resources have been tried and the marital relationship is still unable to heal.

When a married couple encounters difficulties in their relationship, the law continues to support this relationship through various provisions in the Women's Charter. Family Court officials who come into contact with the two parties will continue to remind them of the social services available in Singapore to help them work out their problems so their marriage can possibly continue. It is only when the married couple has reached a stage where it is no longer reasonable to expect them to continue in their marriage that the law offers them the option to end their marriage.

Divorce should not be offered too easily or liberally as this will undermine the institution of marriage. Thus the law of divorce requires a husband or wife to prove that his or her marriage has broken down irretrievably. Further, unless there are exceptional circumstances, a divorce application cannot be made within the first three years of marriage. This restriction aims to ensure that all persons regard marriage with appropriate consideration. No one should rush irresponsibly in or out of marriage. This also means that when there are difficulties in a marital relationship, divorce should not be resorted to until the parties have worked hard at reconciliation and given themselves the time to overcome what could be temporary difficulties. Where, however, divorce is the only way out, the divorce law and processes in the Women's Charter are designed to minimize bitterness, distress and humiliation experienced by the parties, and to achieve a harmonious resolution of the most painful dispute anyone can experience in the course of their lives.

28. How does the law of divorce relate with the law regulating the relationship between husband and wife?

Balance

The availability of divorce is not, in itself, a threat to the institution of marriage. When a couple has truly come to the end of the line, divorce is not necessarily wrong. What is wrong may be for them to divorce before they have reached the end of the line. Loosely worded divorce laws may tend to lead to attitudes where couples divorce too readily and, over time, this may undermine the institution of marriage. There is no such fear where the right balance is achieved. The law in Singapore aims for this balance.

Relates with legal expectations of married persons

The Women's Charter in section 46(1) provides that the husband and wife are equally and mutually bound to cooperate with each other to safeguard the interests of the union (as discussed in Question 13 above). Married partners must, therefore, behave reasonably towards each other. They are given much room to lead their private married lives without constant intervention from the law. Only where the failure to cooperate is extreme will the law of divorce be available to them.

The Women's Charter supports the marital obligations in section 46(1) through its section 49 which imposes a duty on the judge hearing applications for divorce or judicial separation, property disputes between spouses, or family violence and maintenance applications, to consider and encourage reconciliation of the parties. Section 49 is a unique provision of law in that neither party needs to apply to the judge for it to operate. It operates automatically so that every judge who hears a case must follow its direction. When, however, even after assisted reconciliation, a husband or wife considers the failure of the other spouse to cooperate as so extreme that the marriage relationship cannot continue further, he or she may seek the most drastic of court orders, *viz.* a divorce judgement which terminates the relationship.

29. What is the only ground for divorce in Singapore?

One ground

The Women's Charter provides that "either party to a marriage may file a writ for divorce on the ground that the marriage has irretrievably broken down". It, however, demands rigorous proof of the irretrievable breakdown of marriage before the judge will find this state of affairs that allows the judge to terminate the marriage by divorce. The judge shall not consider a marriage to have broken down irretrievably unless he or she is satisfied of one or more of five facts specified in the Women's Charter.

In theory the ground for divorce under the Women's Charter, *viz.* the marriage has irretrievably broken down, does not attribute fault in causing the breakdown to either party to the marriage. Alleging fault and allocating blame on one party may not be conducive to the harmonious resolution of the application and may instead increase acrimony, bitterness, and humiliation. In other words, there is no advantage to be gained by allowing parties to point an accusing finger at each other in their divorce application. The theory is, however, compromised in the requirement of how a spouse proves that his or her marriage has irretrievably broken down.

Five facts

To prove the irretrievable breakdown of the marriage, any of five specified facts can be used as proof. Proof of any of these five facts allows the Family Court to conclude that the marriage in question has irretrievably broken down. Three of the five "facts" still contain one party's "fault" in causing the marital breakdown but two of them are paired with one more element that proves the "irretrievable" character of the breakdown. These three facts are: adultery when it is also shown that the other spouse finds it intolerable to live with him or her; behaviour by one spouse where it is also shown that it is unreasonable to expect the other spouse to continue to cohabit with him or her; and desertion that has continued for a certain number of years. Two of the five "facts" are, however, totally free of any suggestion of the other spouse's "fault" in the failure of the marriage: living apart for three years or for four years. The current divorce law in the Women's Charter is thus a compromise between the "fault-based" grounds under the former divorce law and the newer "no-fault" basis of divorce.

When one of these "facts" is proven, the court will almost always decide that there has been an irretrievable breakdown of the marriage so a divorce can be granted. The court does not question the parties' motivations in seeking to terminate their marriage and only in extremely exceptional cases will a divorce be refused despite proof of one of the "facts". In these extremely exceptional cases the court decides that, despite the irretrievable breakdown of the marriage, it is still "not right" to terminate the marriage. It is hard to imagine when this might come about. One possibility might be where it is proven that a child would be so devastated by his or her parents' divorce that the court may "defer" this until the child is sufficiently prepared for the event. The effect must be truly devastating and beyond the ordinary pain and grief we know all children experience through their parents' divorce. There are no cases in Singapore where the courts have actually refused to grant a divorce after it is proven the marriage has irretrievably broken down.

30. What are the five facts the proof of which allows the court to rule that the marriage has irretrievably broken down?

One party commits adultery and other finds it intolerable to live with him/her

Adultery is committed when a husband or wife voluntarily has sexual intercourse with a person other than his or her spouse. When a husband or wife proves to the court that the other party has committed adultery and he or she finds it intolerable to live with that spouse, the court may hold that the marriage has irretrievably broken down. If adultery is denied by the party alleged to have committed it, the husband or wife seeking to prove it usually hires the services of a private investigator to provide evidence of adultery. The fees for these services can be quite high. Such expense will not be necessary if the alleged spouse admits to adultery. Some parties do not contest a divorce application that includes the allegations of adultery; in these cases a divorce application can proceed uncontested and the cost of obtaining a divorce is kept fairly low.

However, if a husband and wife have lived together for more than six months after the last act of adultery became known to the spouse seeking the divorce, that act of adultery can no longer be relied on as evidence of the irretrievable breakdown of the marriage. The law aims to strike a balance between encouraging attempts at reconciliation and being fair to the party whose past adultery would be deemed to have been forgiven by the other spouse. Such a marriage should be given another chance before it is terminated.

One party behaves in a way so that it is unreasonable to expect the other to continue cohabiting with him/her

When a husband or wife proves to the court that the spouse has behaved in such a way that he or she cannot reasonably be expected to continue to live with that spouse, the court may hold that the marriage has irretrievably broken down. Common allegations of such behaviour include committing physical violence, having frequent quarrels, neglecting the family, not caring or providing for the children, keeping late nights frequently, having the habit of gambling or drinking, and improper associations with other parties. Any and all behaviour which affect the other spouse will be taken into account in the light of all relevant circumstances. Thus where isolated incidents may not be sufficient to prove this fact, a substantial number of small incidents may suffice when the cumulative effect of the incidents is considered.

The court must be satisfied that, objectively, it is unreasonable to expect this particular spouse seeking a divorce to live with his or her spouse. The law supports a couple's attempts at reconciliation so even where the spouses have lived together for short periods after the alleged final incident of behaviour, the fact of their living together is disregarded in determining whether or not the spouse can reasonably be expected to live with the other, provided the total length of their living together after the final incident that supports the allegation does not exceed six months.

One party deserts the other for the past two years

Where one party proves to the court that the other has deserted him or her for at least two years and this continues at the time of the application for divorce, the court may hold the marriage to have irretrievably broken down. A spouse who complains of desertion must prove two elements: that the spouses have lived apart for at least two years and the other spouse had the intention to desert him or her. The spouses will have lived apart if they lived in two separate households. This could mean that the spouses have physically lived in two places of residence, or they could have lived under the same roof but carried on separate lives in two separate households. In the latter situation, there must be sufficient proof that the parties are living in two households, for example, they are not sharing household supplies or assisting each other in household chores. In other words, the question is: are the spouses still sharing their lives or are they just sharing a roof? In the former situation, they are not separated, but in the latter they have separated.

The party who claims to have been deserted must not have agreed to the separation. If he or she agreed to the separation, there is no desertion since the separation is consensual.

There must have been two continuous years of desertion. However, to support attempts at reconciliation, the law treats the period of desertion as continuous even if it was interrupted by one or more periods of resumption of cohabitation, provided that the total length of cohabitation does not exceed six months.

The parties have been living apart for three years (where the one not suing for divorce agrees to the divorce) or living apart for four years (where the other party does not agree to the divorce)

Where the parties have lived apart for three years, and the other party consents to a divorce, the court may find their marriage to have irretrievably broken down. Where the other party does not consent to a divorce, there must be a period of four years of living apart before the court may find that the marriage has irretrievably broken down.

"Living apart" means that the couple does not live in the same household. It is possible for the parties to live under the same roof but still live apart by sleeping in separate bedrooms and keeping separate households where there is no communication, no sharing of a common kitchen and no sharing of household supplies.

While "desertion" involves blameworthiness where one party leaves the other who does not agree to the separation, "living apart" is where the parties live separately by choice. However, parties who live apart by necessity and not by choice are not "living apart" for the purposes of proving the irretrievable breakdown of their marriage.

The law treats the period of "living apart" as continuous even if it was interrupted by one or more periods of resumption of cohabitation, provided that the total length of cohabitation does not exceed six months.

31. How does a husband or wife apply for divorce?

Connection with the Singapore court

The law requires the spouse who seeks the relief of divorce to prove a close connection with the court. The Women's Charter requires either party to the marriage to be either domiciled or habitually resident in Singapore for a period of three years at the commencement of the proceedings. This ensures that the parties involved are sufficiently connected with Singapore. Only then do the courts possess sufficient interest to determine whether the circumstances are right to terminate their marriage.

As long as a person has this connection with the Singapore court, he or she need not have married in Singapore. Even someone married outside Singapore under a marriage law different from the Women's Charter may form the necessary connection with Singapore to become entitled to apply for divorce in Singapore.

Among Singaporeans, however, this part of the Women's Charter is only open to persons married under the Women's Charter. Muslim persons married under Muslim law must use the equivalent Muslim law of divorce.

Court documents

The divorce proceedings start with the filing of a Writ for Divorce. The party seeking the divorce is called the "Plaintiff" and the other party, the "Defendant". The Writ for Divorce, together with the Statement of Claim and the Statement of Particulars, must be filed electronically by the Plaintiff through the Electronic Filing System (the "EFS"). The Statement of Claim should state the fact which shows the irretrievable breakdown of the marriage such as adultery, behaviour, desertion, or living apart. The Statement of Particulars should give details of the fact relied on, such as instances of behaviour that make it unreasonable to expect the plaintiff to continue to cohabit with the defendant. If there are children from the marriage, a Parenting Plan must also be filed (discussed in Question 34 below). Further, if there is a Housing and Development Board ("HDB") flat to be divided between the parties should the divorce be granted, a Matrimonial Property Plan (discussed also in Question 34 below) must be filed as well. After the court accepts the documents filed, the sealed documents must be served on the defendant.

Contested or not

The divorce proceedings may take one of two forms: it is either contested or uncontested. If the defendant denies the allegations made by the plaintiff and contests the divorce, a contested divorce hearing will ensue which takes more time and can turn costly. The divorce process is also likely to be more distressing, acrimonious and even humiliating for one or both parties involved. Uncontested divorces, on the other hand, involve less time and costs. They also reduce the opportunities for parties to repeat allegations against each other as the allegations are confined to those already set out in the Statement of Particulars. Mediation (discussed in Question 32 below) is a process which can guide the parties towards obtaining a divorce on an uncontested basis.

32. How does mediation help in the harmonious resolution of the application for divorce?

Mediation

The Women's Charter describes one role of the Family Court as encouraging the harmonious resolution of family disputes through the processes of mediation and counselling. Where there are children from the marriage who are minors, parents must continue to remain responsible parents who are able to cooperate in parenting their children even after the divorce. The divorce law and processes aim to ensure that the marriage is ended with the minimum of acrimony and bitterness. This is vital in ensuring that there is the chance the parties can continue to cooperate as parents for the welfare of their children.

Mediation in family disputes is offered in-house by the Family Court at the Family Resolution Chambers. In Family Mediation (lawyers call this a "Resolution Conference" in the Family Court), parties agree to have the Family Resolution judge or mediator assist them in reaching an informed settlement by negotiation instead of adjudication. Discussions during mediation are confidential and parties are not bound by the initial offers made during mediation. Should mediation fail to result in a settlement and the case proceeds to a full hearing in court, the judge hearing the case has no access to information offered during the mediation.

Benefits of mediation

As mediation aims to help parties reach a solution that meets the needs of both parties and their children, there need not be a "winner" or "loser" emerging from these court proceedings. It is believed that parties feel happier with terms they have agreed on rather than terms imposed on them by a court adjudicated order. Mediation also saves much time and legal costs. Parties are spared the distress and trauma of going through a contested hearing which can potentially increase tension and acrimony. In fact, mediation may improve communications between the parties and both parties retain greater control of the case than when the matter is adjudicated by a judge. Each party can be advised to negotiate for what is most important to him or her in exchange for something subjectively less important. As family disputes can be complicated, involving intimate relationships that have broken down, it is generally desirable that parties sort out arrangements for the future on their own.

33. What community assistance — legal and non-legal — is available to a couple going through a divorce?

Counselling

The Women's Charter places on the judge hearing an application for divorce the duty to consider the possibility of reconciliation between the parties and to make directions and orders appropriate to achieving this. Within the Family Court, the Family and Juvenile Justice Centre offers in-house counselling to assist in the harmonious resolution of family disputes. There are various forms of counselling with each having its own objective.

"Reconciliation counselling" is offered to spouses who are willing to attempt reconciliation to save the marriage, or who are unsure whether they really want to be divorced. "Conciliation counselling" is offered where one spouse is resolute about getting a divorce while the other spouse needs some help in coming to terms with the impending divorce. It assists the spouse to accept the breakdown of the marriage and deal with related emotional issues. It can be said that reconciliation counselling works at "marriage mending" and conciliation counselling assists the parties to work towards an amicable "marriage ending". In assisting spouses to achieve a holistically amicable divorce, conciliation counselling is also offered to assist spouses in making custody, care and control, and access arrangements which best serve the children's welfare. "Support counselling" is also available to help children who are affected by their parents' divorce.

Community support resources are also widely available at the Family Service Centres situated in various geographical locations in Singapore. There are more than thirty Family Service Centres in Singapore, all partially funded by the Ministry of Community Development, Youth and Sports and the National Council of Social Services. Members of the public may seek support services for family-related issues at these centres which are manned by social workers and counsellors. Apart from Family Service Centres, there are also counselling services offered by private practitioners who assist in marriage mending and amicable marriage ending.

Legal assistance

Parties who are Singapore citizens or permanent residents with little or no income may seek legal assistance at the Legal Aid Bureau. Legal aid is available to parties with limited means in the form of legal advice, legal assistance in drafting simple documents, and legal representation in simple matters such as those arising from family proceedings. There is also a recently established *Pro Bono* Services

Office at the Subordinate Courts of Singapore. Parties can seek legal assistance from one of the Community Legal Clinics run by the *Pro Bono* Services Office of the Law Society of Singapore. General legal advice is also available at the Legal Clinic which operates twice a month at the Family and Juvenile Court Building.

Parties who are not eligible for legal aid at the Legal Aid Bureau will need to instruct a lawyer or represent herself or himself in the proceedings. It is advisable that a lawyer experienced in family practice be instructed as family practice is unique and requires a less adversarial strategy as well as familiarity with specialized rules customized for family disputes. Effective family lawyering is an art. A good family practitioner will help the client achieve what he or she seeks but, at the same time, try to keep the relationship between the spouses as amicable as possible so that they can continue to discharge their parental responsibilities towards their children with minimal disruption.

34. What other processes assist former spouses in resolving financial matters and the living arrangements of their children now that they will no longer live together?

Apart from the resources of mediation and counselling (discussed in Question 33 above), the Women's Charter (Matrimonial Proceedings) Rules provide for procedures and rules that help the parties resolve related matters (lawyers call these "ancillary matters") upon their divorce.

If there are children in the family, a Parenting Plan must be filed together with the Writ for Divorce, the

Statement of Claim, and the Statement of Particulars. An Agreed Parenting Plan is filed if both parties are able to agree on the living arrangements of their children after their divorce. Where the parents cannot agree, the spouse applying for the divorce will submit his or her Proposed Parenting Plan. The Parenting Plan compels the divorcing spouses to think through their parental responsibilities to their children. Divorce ends the shared household and the law expects parents to consider carefully future arrangements that will promote the welfare of the children affected by the breakup of the family household. The court is also assisted by the information contained in the Parenting Plan when it has to make orders regarding the children's living arrangements (discussed in Question 21 above).

If there is a Housing and Development Board ("HDB") flat to be divided between the spouses should a divorce be granted, a Matrimonial Property Plan must be filed. A "standard query" is submitted to the HDB which will give responses advising the parties on the various options they have with respect to the HDB flat in question. The information given by the HDB enables the parties to consider realistically whether their HDB flat can be kept, sold, or divided between themselves in just and equitable proportions. The Matrimonial Property Plan also usefully gives the court guidance in determining how the HDB asset should be divided or dealt with upon the divorce (discussed in Question 41 below).

The law and processes require parties to disclose fully their assets (discussed in Question 46 below). Parties will be required to file a document (lawyers call this an "affidavit of assets and means") where this is appropriate. The law puts some pressure on the spouses to make full disclosure by allowing the court to draw adverse inferences against the party who, in the court's judgement, has not been completely frank in disclosing his or her assets and means.

VII   MAINTENANCE

35. Who owes the duty to provide reasonable maintenance to a child?

Parents primarily, other adults secondarily

The Women's Charter imposes the duty to provide maintenance to a child dependent on financial support primarily on the parents. Where a parent or both parents are proven to have failed to discharge their responsibility when they are able to do so (discussed in Question 17 above), the Family Court is empowered to make an order to the parent(s) to provide a specified amount for the child's reasonable maintenance.

If, however, the parents are not discharging their duty and, instead, some adult has voluntarily assumed the responsibility of providing this financial support by accepting the dependent child as a member of his or her own family, the Family Court is empowered to order this adult to continue to provide a specified amount for the child's reasonable maintenance. Where the parents of a child can be held responsible for his or her financial needs, there is no reason for the Family Court to impose this responsibility on any other adult. Where the parents fail, the court may turn to the adult who has accepted the child as a member of his or her family.

The Family Court first enforces parental responsibility and will only impose the extension of this on an adult who is not a parent of the child where it is not possible to hold the parents to their responsibility.

Reasonable maintenance

The Women's Charter directs the Family Court to take all relevant factors into consideration in deciding how much maintenance is reasonable for the particular child. These include the financial needs of the child, the income and earning capacity of the person to be ordered to pay, any disability of the child that may raise the particular child's needs, the standard of living enjoyed by the child up to the time of the application, and the manner in which the child is expected to be educated or trained for employment.

Age

Maintenance is normally ordered for a child until he or she reaches the age of twenty-one years. The Women's Charter exceptionally allows for maintenance to be ordered beyond the age of twenty-one where there are good reasons for it. Good reasons include the child suffering some mental or physical disability, the child serving or will be serving full-time national service, the child receiving or will be receiving instruction in an educational establishment or undergoing training for a trade, profession or vocation, or for any other "special circumstances".

Who can apply for the child?

Either the child himself (if he or she has already reached the age of twenty-one and is able to initiate legal proceedings), or an adult who has custody of the child, or a grown sibling of the child, or even an administrative official appointed by the Minister for Community Development, Youth and Sports for the general care of dependent children in Singapore, may make the application on behalf of the child. The

Women's Charter has provided mechanisms to assist a dependent child in overcoming legal incapacity owing to youth in seeking the provision of reasonable maintenance for himself or herself. The child's application is made against a parent or, where this is appropriate, an adult who has accepted the child as a member of his or her family; in either case the person who will be ordered to pay is the "defendant" in the child's application.

Not limited to Singaporean children

The provision in the Women's Charter is broad and is not limited to children who are Singaporeans, or of parents who are Singaporeans. It is also one of the provisions in the Women's Charter that applies to both Muslims and non-Muslims. In theory, anyone in the world can begin an application in Singapore for a maintenance order for a child as long as he and the child are physically present at the application. Practically speaking, however, no foreigner will aim to do this unless the person to be ordered to pay either lives and works here or has financial resources here. If not for this, it makes no sense for foreigners to obtain a maintenance order from Singapore's Family Court although in theory this is possible to do.

36. How is the duty of a parent to maintain a child related with parental responsibility?

Directly enforceable responsibility

The duty of a parent to provide reasonable maintenance is one specific parental responsibility (discussed in Question 17 above) that is directly enforced by the Family Court. A parent who fails in discharging this responsibility towards his or her child has failed so abjectly that the courts will intervene in their relationship by making an order to the parent to pay a specified amount towards the maintenance of the child.

Father and mother equally liable

Both father and mother are equally liable to provide reasonable maintenance to a dependent child. Who between them would be subjected to the Family Court's maintenance order depends simply on who has not been making reasonable provision (and so needs to be ordered by the court to do so), or who is financially capable of meeting the order. Parental responsibility falls equally on the father and the mother of the child, so this one aspect of it also falls as much on the father as on the mother.

Irrelevant whether living with child

A father or mother may be ordered by the Family Court to make reasonable provision for the maintenance of the dependent child whether the child lives with him or her. The child may even be living with someone else (*eg.* a grandparent or aunt or uncle or even a family friend) and a financially capable parent can still be ordered to pay. Parental responsibility is tenacious and survives any change in the living arrangements of the family members.

Whether legitimate

It is not only a legitimate child (*ie.*, a child born to parents who were validly married to each other at the time of the child's birth) who can obtain a maintenance order against his or her parents. The Women's Charter provides that the duty rests on the parents whether their relationship with their child falls within the description of being "legitimate" or not. This aspect of parental responsibility that may be regarded as of the highest practical importance is imposed on the parents whether they had their child within marriage or outside marriage.

Irrelevant whether parents are divorced

Where the parents of the child were married to each other at some time it is completely irrelevant whether their marriage remains subsisting or has since ended in divorce. The termination of marriage by divorce has a devastating effect on the spouses' relationship with each other but it has no effect whatsoever on their relationship with their child. The parent-child relationship is intact even though the parents are divorced. More importantly, parental responsibility remains intact (as discussed in Question 17 above).

The duty of the parents to provide reasonable maintenance for their financially dependent child is exactly the same during the subsistence of their marriage or after its termination. This legal regulation of the relationship between parents and their child or children is very clearly expressed in the Women's Charter. There is only one set of provisions spelling out the duty of parents to provide reasonable maintenance for their child or children. The same provisions apply whether the Family Court is enforcing them during the continuance of the parents' marriage, or after their divorce, or even after the husband or wife or both have remarried. The law continues to hold them to their responsibilities to all their children. Of course, if one or both parents have other children with another person, this fact will have to be reflected in the Family Court's assessment of what constitutes a reasonable maintenance order for the child concerned in the maintenance application.

37. Who, between a husband and wife, has the duty to provide reasonable maintenance to the other?

Marital partners

As marital partners cooperating for their mutual benefit, both husband and wife should mutually have the duty to provide reasonable maintenance to one another. The Women's Charter, however, has since its enactment in 1961, only made the husband responsible for providing reasonable maintenance to his dependent wife. Upon divorce, the husband may still be ordered to continue providing reasonable maintenance to his dependent former wife. In any such application the husband who may be ordered to pay is the "defendant".

A capable wife has no duty to provide reasonable maintenance to her dependent husband. While it is still true that it is normally the wife who is financially dependent and a dependent husband may well be an infrequent exception to the rule, it is nevertheless a flaw of the Women's Charter that it has not yet equalized the duty of maintenance between spouses. It would be a better law that is more in synch with the moral message to spouses that they are engaging in an equal cooperative partnership of different efforts (discussed in Question 13 above) were the duty of maintenance between spouses imposed as much on the capable wife as on the capable husband. While this flaw has already been pointed out, the authorities do not feel it is time to correct it yet partly because the situation where a husband is dependent on his wife for maintenance remains a rare exception.

During marriage

During the subsistence of a marriage a wife may prove to the Family Court that her husband, despite her needing it and his being capable of doing so, has failed or neglected to provide her with reasonable maintenance. On being proven these facts, the Family Court can make an order to the husband specifying the amount he should provide for his wife's reasonable maintenance. The court will take all relevant factors into consideration in assessing what is reasonable maintenance for the wife.

Not limited to women married under the Women's Charter

The provision in the Women's Charter that allows the Family Court to make a maintenance order for a wife is not limited to women who are married under the Women's Charter. The provision is one of those that applies to persons married under Muslim law whether of Singapore or abroad. Indeed any woman who is validly married under a marriage law anywhere in the world may apply for this. Practically speaking, however, it is only where the husband lives and works in Singapore or has financial resources in Singapore that his wife will make an application in Singapore. Except for this, it makes little sense for a foreigner to apply to

Singapore's Family Court for a maintenance order although this is possible to do.

Upon divorce

The Family Court can order a capable husband to continue to provide reasonable maintenance to his wife upon the termination of their marriage by divorce. The scenario upon divorce is, of course, completely different from that during the subsistence of a functioning marriage, and the law responds to these differences appropriately. Upon divorce, the Family Court approaches the matter of maintenance of the wife in conjunction with another order that the court might make between the parties *viz.*, an order for the division of their matrimonial assets (discussed in Part VIII below). While the Women's Charter gives the Family Court a free hand, it appears more likely than not that an order for the division of matrimonial assets will usually be made first. An order of maintenance supplements the order for the division of matrimonial assets. The simple explanation for this is that, where the parties have property to divide, it is better for this to be ordered divided between them before the Family Court considers whether it is necessary for a further order of maintenance to be made.

Maintenance of a divorced wife

Where the order of maintenance is necessary the Family Court will, as always, consider all relevant factors in deciding what would be reasonable maintenance and for how long.

As the couple's marital relationship has come to an end, there are factors for consideration that are only relevant in this scenario. As said above, maintenance of a divorced wife should be assessed together with the order for the division of matrimonial assets. The Family Court will see if it is possible for the maintenance to be ordered to be paid in one lump sum or several instalments rather than on a periodical basis. There may be an agreement that the spouses had made regarding the amount of maintenance the divorced wife should receive and this will be given some consideration although the court is not bound to order according to the agreement unless it regards the amount agreed on as fair and reasonable. The court will consider the duration of the marriage and the contributions both spouses made to the marriage during its subsistence. The court will expect the divorced wife to try to regain her own financial self-sufficiency and will assess her ability to achieve this.

In the end, what is ordered is what is considered fair to expect of the man in continuing to provide for his former wife, and for how long after they have already voluntarily terminated their relationship by divorce.

Duration of maintenance of divorced wife

An order to a man to continue to provide reasonable maintenance to his divorced wife ends when the Family Court orders it to end or, alternatively, it ends when either the husband or wife dies, or when the wife remarries. Upon her remarriage, it is her new husband who assumes the duty to provide her with reasonable maintenance.

Award of maintenance to divorced wife limited to Singapore divorces

As the power of the Family Court to order the husband, upon divorce, to continue to maintain his former wife is one of the powers unique to a court when its power to give a judgement of divorce is invoked, this power is not accessible unless the judgement of divorce was granted in Singapore. Where a Singaporean is divorced overseas, the Family Court is not allowed to make a maintenance order in favour of the divorced wife. She is expected to go back to the court that granted the divorce to obtain a maintenance order.

38. What is the goal of the Family Court in making an award of maintenance?

The Women's Charter directs the Family Court to aim to balance all the considerations that present themselves in any application for a maintenance order. The considerations that may assume the greatest significance could be the financial needs of the applicant, on the one hand, and the capability of the defendant (*ie.*, the person who is ordered to pay) on the other. The goal is always what appears to be reasonable when all relevant factors are considered.

In the case of the maintenance of a divorced wife, there could be important additional considerations such as encouraging the divorced woman to try to regain her financial self-sufficiency as, at some point, she should no longer be able to ask for money from the man who once used to be her husband.

39. How is an order of maintenance enforced?

Ideal

The ideal is where the defendant (*ie.*, the person who is ordered to pay) meets the payments required of him or her without the need for enforcement. This is where the Women's Charter encouragement of less acrimony during family proceedings assumes significance. Where a maintenance order is made at the conclusion of amicable family proceedings in court, there is every hope that the defendant will meet his or her obligations without the need for legal enforcement.

Several mechanisms

Where, unfortunately, legal enforcement becomes necessary, the Women's Charter offers several mechanisms for enforcement. The Women's Charter allows the Family Court, upon proof of every breach of a maintenance order, to direct that the sum owing should be levied in the same way a fine may be levied when an offence is committed, or that the defaulter should be sentenced to imprisonment for a term no longer than one month for every month's allowance remaining unpaid. Alternatively, it may order a person who owes money to the defaulter to pay the sum owing to the child or wife for whose benefit the maintenance order was made. In other words, the Women's Charter adopts the means of enforcement of judgements at the conclusion of civil suits, or sentences at the conclusion of criminal trials, which are appropriate to use in enforcing maintenance orders. It should also be remembered that each unpaid maintenance is a debt owed by the defendant (*ie.*, the person ordered to pay) to the plaintiff (*ie.*, the child or wife for whose benefit the maintenance order was made) of the maintenance order. In theory then, the plaintiff can sue the defendant for any outstanding sum, just as he or she can sue any debtor.

Attachment of earnings order

The most practical enforcement mechanism may be where the court makes an additional order to "attach" the earnings of the defendant. This order is directed to the defendant's employer who is authorised by the court to deduct the amount ordered as maintenance from the employee's salary and pay this sum of money directly to an official of the court. The court will then redirect this sum to the child or wife who was ordered to receive this amount of maintenance. As the employer deducts the money "at source" this can be quite effective. The mechanism, however, is only available where the defendant is employed. For the unemployed or self-employed the mechanism will not be available or as effective.

Enforcement outside the country where the order was made

It is possible for a maintenance order made outside Singapore to be enforced by the courts as if it were made in Singapore, just as it is possible for a maintenance order made in Singapore to be enforced by the courts of another country.

The child or wife will seek to do this where the defendant has moved to another country and is now earning income there. Singapore enters into bilateral agreements with other countries to allow for the reciprocal enforcement of one another's maintenance orders. To date this has been achieved with a few countries (mainly, its nearest neighbour Malaysia and Commonwealth countries) and more countries may be added in time.

40. What is the responsibility of an adult child for the maintenance of his or her aged dependent parent?

The Women's Charter is supplemented by the Maintenance of Parents Act (Chapter 167B of the 1996 Revised Edition of the Statutes of the Republic of Singapore) that allows a tribunal to order an adult child who is capable of providing maintenance to maintain his or her aged (*ie.*, at least over sixty years old) dependent (*ie.*, not financially self-sufficient) parent. A tribunal is a semi-judicial body. It is not the same as the Family Court. The members of the Tribunal of Maintenance of Parents are not judges although most of them are legally qualified.

This responsibility is somewhat secondary to the adult child's responsibility to his own wife and children since the adult child's liability towards his own wife and children is one factor the tribunal will take into consideration. The responsibility is also somewhat dependent on the parent having discharged his or her parental responsibility towards the adult child when he or she was younger and dependent. This is because the tribunal is required to consider whether there has been such a failure of parental responsibility that no order would be made for the aged dependent parent. Where the aged dependent parent has several capable adult children the tribunal is empowered to divide the responsibility of providing maintenance among the siblings as it sees fit.

VIII DIVISION OF MATRIMONIAL ASSETS

41. What does the Women's Charter allow of the matrimonial assets of a couple upon their divorce?

Section 112(1)

The Women's Charter in section 112(1) gives the Family Court a very broad discretionary power to make an order that divides the parties' matrimonial assets between them in just and equitable proportions. This power arises only upon the termination of their marriage by a judgement of court.

The power was enacted and added to the Women's Charter in 1980 (although at that time it was section 106). The enactment of this law was a remarkably bold step the Parliament of Singapore took in 1980. A power of this nature stems from a view of the acquisition of property by spouses during marriage that was originally associated with countries that belong to the "civil law" family of legal systems (*eg.* France or Sweden). Singapore (just like England) belongs to the alternative "common law" family of legal systems which held a different view of the acquisition of property by spouses. Even today England still does not have a statutory provision that is worded quite as boldly as Singapore's Women's Charter's section 112. However, as the idea behind section 112 has become widely accepted as the fair way to treat spouses' property upon their divorce, the House of Lords — now called the Supreme Court of England (the highest court in England) — decided in 2000 that English courts should also exercise their power to achieve a fair distribution of the property that divorced parties own at their divorce. In other words, Singaporeans can note with some pride that our law in this respect developed ahead of the law in England by about twenty years.

No similar power during the subsistence of marriage

The significance of the power to order the division of matrimonial assets of a couple upon divorce can be appreciated when one remembers what the common law rule is regarding ownership of property between a husband and wife during the course of their marriage. Family law in Singapore (like that in England) leaves the regulation of property between a husband and wife completely to the general principles of property law. Family law does not provide special principles for the married couple.

The effect of this is that the existence of a marital relationship between a husband and wife has little relevance when one spouse has a dispute with the other over ownership of property. The dispute between a husband and wife is settled using the same principles as a dispute between persons who are not married to each other. Property law mainly recognizes the payment of money as the means by which a person acquires ownership of property. The wife, by doing what a wife normally does for the well-being of the family and caring for the children, does not gain ownership of property paid for by the husband. Similarly, if it were the husband who was doing the household chores while the wife worked and paid for the property, the husband would not gain ownership of property. The Family Court does not possess the power to divide a couple's property between them during the subsistence of their marriage.

Upon the termination of their marriage, however, the Women's Charter in section 112(1) gives the Family Court a wide discretionary power to take all relevant considerations into account to order a division of property that are "matrimonial assets" in proportions that are just and equitable. This family law principle is much more in tune with family dynamics where one spouse usually concentrates on making money and the other concentrates on homemaking and child caring. The family law view allows the courts to give equal credit to both kinds of efforts made by the spouses during the course of their marriage.

The difference between the law that applies during the subsistence of a marriage and that which applies upon termination of that marriage is very stark.

Deferred community of property

Another way of making the same point is that the law in Singapore subscribes to the concept of "deferred community of property".

"Community of property" is an idea that came from the civil law family of legal systems. The idea here is that any property that is acquired by either the husband or the wife is immediately owned by both of them so that a "community" is created of all their property. This idea stands in contrast with that of the common law family of legal systems where marriage has minimal effect on property acquired. The common law view is that the property is acquired by the party who paid for the property. It follows from this that if the other party did not also pay for a part of it, being the spouse of the owner of the property does not entitle him or her to any part of it. The law in Singapore (as in England) continues to subscribe to this view while the parties are still married to each other. Upon their divorce, however, a completely different view is introduced by the Women's Charter section 112.

By enacting the power in the Family Court to order the just and equitable division of matrimonial assets upon divorce in the Women's Charter section 112, the law in Singapore has embraced the community of property view, but deferred it until the marriage is terminated in divorce. That is why the law in Singapore since 1980 (and since 2000 in England) conforms to the concept of "deferred community of property".

Deferred community of property widely accepted as ideal balance

Many countries in the common law family of legal systems as well as in the civil law family of legal systems have come to accept the concept of "deferred community of property" as the ideal way of regulating property disputes between spouses. "Deferred community of property" is an improvement over "community of property" as the latter is recognized to be unduly cumbersome. Under "community of property" any person who proposes to buy property will need to check if the owner is a married person and, where married, will need to deal both with the owner, and his or her spouse who automatically also has entitlement to the property by virtue of being the spouse of the owner.

By deferring this until the couple divorces, the concept of "deferred community of property" preserves the ease of transactions over property that is vital in a vibrant economy. "Deferred community of property" gives the Family Court an opportunity upon the termination of the couple's marriage to look into their property holdings and divide matrimonial assets so that each party receives a just and equitable proportion thereof. The concept achieves both the aim of allowing the market economy to run smoothly and the aim that both the party who paid for the matrimonial asset as well as the other party would be fairly treated upon their divorce. It is about as close to the ideal as the people who think about the law can come up with.

42. How well does the idea of "deferred community of property" relate with the view of marriage as the spouses' "equal cooperative partnership of different efforts"?

It was said in Question 13 that the Women's Charter through its section 46(1) describes marriage as the spouses' equal cooperative partnership of different efforts for their mutual benefit. The concept of "deferred community of property" relates perfectly with this view of marriage. It is exactly because a husband and wife bring different efforts into their marital partnership that the law should regard both of them as having contributed equally to acquiring the property that one of them may have paid for during the course of their marriage. It ought not matter whether it was the husband or the wife who paid for the property while the other's contribution was "non-financial". Each contribution, whether financial or non-financial, was equally valuable to the well-being of their marital partnership. The spouse who made the financial contribution will very likely not have been able to do so if not for the fact that he or she benefitted from the other making non-financial contribution.

Where today it is more usual for both husband and wife to make financial contributions to the acquisition of property during their marriage, it should not greatly matter what the size of their respective financial contributions was. Since both husband and wife are engaging in an equal cooperative partnership, the law should regard their contributions as being more or less of equal value. The idea of deferred community of property gives the court the broad discretionary power to assign this equal value to whatever efforts the husband and wife made to their marriage.

43. What is the aim of the court when it makes an order for the division of the couple's matrimonial assets between them?

Just and equitable proportions

The Women's Charter in section 112(1) directs the Family Court very generally to aim for a division of the matrimonial assets between a divorced husband and wife in proportions the court deems just and equitable.

To be fair to both

The idea of this direction is for the order of division to be fair to both parties. Neither party is favoured. Neither financial nor non-financial contribution that each party may have made is favoured. Both parties and all the contributions each has made find equal favour with the courts. In exercising its power to divide matrimonial assets in just and equitable proportions, the Family Court holds both parties firmly to their commitment to cooperate equally within their marital partnership of different efforts for mutual benefit. Precisely because they were equal partners, the excess wealth and assets of the partnership (which matrimonial assets may generally be regarded as) should be divided between them in just and equitable proportions.

Quotable quotes

It is worthwhile to quote the former Singapore Chief Justice in a famous decision in which he said: *"We are of the opinion that [section 112] gives the court a very wide power to order the division of matrimonial assets in the fairest way possible between the parties."* A judge of the High Court in another famous decision said: *"The enactments are meant, in my view, to provide for a just apportionment for the 'homemaker' (invariably the wife) even though the assets under dispute were acquired during the marriage by the sole effort of the other spouse, having regard to the contributions made by the 'homemaker' by looking after the home, caring for the family and the needs of the minor children."*

44. How does the court's power to divide matrimonial assets upon a couple's divorce in just and equitable proportions affirm the equal value of the different efforts spouses make during marriage?

Equal value

The fact that the Family Court is empowered to achieve a just and equitable division of a couple's matrimonial assets upon their divorce says that the law truly accords equal value to all kinds of efforts a husband and wife made during their marriage. It is a fact of life that husband and wife have different strengths and weaknesses so that each one brings different efforts into the marriage. The law should not differentiate between these efforts however different they may be. It should not give greater importance to one kind of effort over another because all of these efforts were needed for the marriage to be successful in acquiring as much wealth and assets as it did.

Neutral

How a husband and wife divide their roles during marriage is a matter truly of their own private concern. The law should remain completely neutral to their decision. It follows that the law should accord equal value to each party's roles. This is the moral message conveyed by the Women's Charter section 112.

Quotable quote

In a recent decision a judge in Singapore's Court of Appeal said: *"It is therefore the duty of the court to recognize the reality of family dynamics and give due weight to all indirect contributions of the other party which are by nature not reducible to monetary terms."* The moral message within section 112 of the Women's Charter reaffirms the moral message within section 46(1) (discussed in Question 13 above). Through these two provisions the Women's Charter tells a couple: cooperate during marriage for your mutual benefit and, when you do terminate your marital partnership, each of you should obtain a just and equitable share of the matrimonial assets that are left.

45. What is a matrimonial asset?

Section 112(10)

The broad discretionary power of the Family Court to order the just and equitable division of property between a husband and wife upon their divorce is only exercisable over "matrimonial assets". Thus only specific property comes under this power. The Women's Charter section 112 in its subsection (10) provides a definition of matrimonial assets that is fairly broad. The idea behind it comes from a famous decision of the High Court in 1989 where it said that property of any kind that was acquired during the course of the marriage is matrimonial asset unless there is a good reason to exclude it.

Seeks two connections

A property is matrimonial asset if it has two connections with the marriage and the parties. One, it should be connected in time with the marriage. Thus, property acquired during the course of the marriage is generally matrimonial asset while property acquired before the marriage needs to have been brought into the marital relationship by the person who acquired it. Property acquired after termination of marriage by divorce is clearly not matrimonial asset. Two, it should be connected with the personal efforts of either the husband or the wife. Thus, property paid for by their own money or work is generally matrimonial asset, while property acquired by windfall (*eg*. as a gift or through inheritance) is not matrimonial asset unless it was brought into the marital relationship by the spouse who was given the property or who inherited it.

Property of any kind acquired during the marriage

Of property acquired during the course of the marriage, all kinds of property are included as matrimonial asset and thus subject to the court's power to divide. This includes the matrimonial home as well as everything else bought for the use of the family and its members. Where the matrimonial home is an HDB flat, the party seeking a divorce must file a Matrimonial Property Plan where information is provided on how much each party paid towards the purchase price including monthly instalment payments as well as towards the monthly conservancy fees for maintenance of the property (discussed in Question 34 above). Property bought for investment, whether these are in Singapore or abroad, are included. All manner of employment remuneration (not just the salary) are included. The courts in Singapore readily take into account the spouses' Central Provident Fund ("CPF") money balance, including investments or property bought with CPF monies, as matrimonial asset. This is despite the fact that it may be possible to regard the CPF account as meant for the employee's personal financial needs upon his or her retirement. Courts in Singapore developed the principle fairly early on. The courts in England today are also permitted to distribute pension rights between former spouses. The courts in Singapore also have no difficulty including modern remuneration benefits, such as stock options, within matrimonial assets. The only property acquired during marriage that is not classified as matrimonial assets is that acquired as a gift to one spouse only, or through inheritance by one spouse, but, as can be seen immediately below, even these may exceptionally be included as well.

Gift or inheritance

The definition of matrimonial assets excludes a property acquired as gift to one party only, or through inheritance by one party only, whether this acquisition was during the course of the marriage or before the marriage. The definition, however, allows the gifted or inherited property to become matrimonial asset by either of, at least, two ways.

One, if the gifted or inherited property was allowed to be used by the family as their matrimonial home, the property becomes a matrimonial asset and subject to the court's power to divide it. Two, if the gifted or inherited property was substantially improved (in physical condition or in value) by the personal efforts of the other party or by both parties during their marriage, the property becomes matrimonial asset and subject to the court's power to divide it. It is therefore possible even for property that is generally excluded from the definition of matrimonial asset to be re-included by use of one of these arguments. The point is that either argument connects the gifted or inherited property sufficiently to the time of the marriage and the personal efforts of a husband and wife so that it is part of the partnership wealth and so should be divided in just and equitable proportions upon their divorce.

Property acquired before the marriage

Property that either the husband or wife acquired before he or she became married is generally not matrimonial asset as it lacks a connection with the marriage. It can, however, acquire sufficient connection by one of two arguments.

One, just as with gifted or inherited property, if the premarital property was substantially improved (in physical condition or in value) by the personal efforts of the other party or by both parties during their marriage, the property becomes matrimonial asset and subject to the court's power to divide it. Two, if the party who acquired the premarital property allowed it to be used by the family the property also becomes matrimonial asset and subject to the court's power to divide it.

Value

The courts do not physically divide up the matrimonial assets between the divorced parties. What is divided is the value of the matrimonial assets. The courts will accept evidence provided as to what is the current value of each piece of property that meets with the definition of a matrimonial asset. They will then deduct the part of this value that does not belong to either party. For example, where the matrimonial asset is still being paid off by a bank loan, this loan is deducted so that what is left is the net value of the matrimonial asset that is truly owned by either or both parties at the time of their divorce. It is the net value of the whole group of properties that are considered matrimonial assets which will be divided in just and equitable proportions between the divorced parties.

46. How would the Family Court obtain all relevant financial information in order to judge what is just and equitable division?

The law regards both parties involved in the application for an order of the just and equitable division of their matrimonial assets as having the duty to make "full and frank disclosure". This means that both husband and wife must provide the Family Court with all the relevant information, particularly pertaining to his or her financial situation, present and past, as well as full information on all properties he or she has a share in, including when and how it was acquired, and what income and expenses are associated with each property. Judges have in the past made it clear that they take this duty of the parties to make full and frank disclosure very seriously. Where there is a reasonable suspicion that a party has failed in discharging this duty it owes to the court, the court has the power to make its disapproval known. The court may judge it fair to make an adverse inference against the party whom it suspects to have failed to make full and frank disclosure. This rule, to some extent, ensures that it does not pay for a husband or wife to try to keep relevant information away from the judge of the Family Court. His or her best chance of a judgement that reflects a just and equitable division of the matrimonial assets is to make full disclosure to the court.

47. What has been the pattern of orders of division of matrimonial assets that Singapore courts have made?

The courts in Singapore have made remarkable orders of division of matrimonial assets during the thirty years that this law has been in existence. While the law allows the Family Court to make orders of any proportion including 1:99, it may be fair to say that a large majority of the orders made fall in the range of 35:65. Where the marriage lasted a long time before the divorce, for example, twenty years or so, the courts are perfectly comfortable ordering an equal division (50:50) for the divorced husband and wife.

It is not unfair to say that an order is fairly likely to be of equal division of the matrimonial assets, or within a fairly narrow range from equal division. It is not possible to be any more specific in predicting what will be decided as the just and equitable proportions of division as this is only arrived at after considering all relevant factors.

48. Can the law in Singapore on division of matrimonial assets claim to be among her finest laws?

Several justifications

There are several justifications for regarding the law on division of matrimonial assets as among the finest law in Singapore.

Early among common law countries

When Parliament first enacted the power in the Family Court to make an order of division of matrimonial assets in 1980, this move was very bold since there were few examples within the common law family of legal systems to which Singapore belongs that had done the same. Today, thirty years later, many more countries have seen the benefit and fairness in the approach that the Singapore Parliament appreciated and adopted before others did.

Raises value of homemaking and childcaring

The power in the Family Court to order the just and equitable division of matrimonial assets raises the value of homemaking and childcaring. The principles of property law (that were developed with property disputes between strangers as the norm) do not accord value to homemaking and childcaring. The party who performs these roles for however long a period will not acquire ownership of a property that has been paid for by the other party. Ignoring homemaking and childcaring is largely fair where the dispute is not between a husband and wife. However, if the law were to continue to ignore homemaking and childcaring where the dispute is between a husband and wife, this would allow one party to gain an unfair advantage over the other. Only the party who assumes the breadwinning role will get to keep all the property he or she paid for during the marriage and the fact that he or she could pay for all these properties partly because the other party took care of the homemaking and childcaring is ignored. One party gains and the other loses simply due to the role he or she discharged during the marriage.

By the Women's Charter section 112 the family law principle corrects such an imbalance at the point of divorce. By doing so it raises the value of homemaking and childcaring to be equal, or close to equal, with the value of breadwinning. This is right. It is fair to both and does not favour one role at the expense of the other.

Raises value of work women normally do

In raising the value of homemaking and childcaring, this family law principle also has an incidental effect. It just so happens that homemaking and childcaring is the sort of work normally discharged by women. This does not have to be so and men may be beginning to make greater contributions to homemaking and childcaring. It will, however, take a long time before the normal pattern of most families changes significantly. For the foreseeable future, homemaking and childcaring will continue to be largely discharged by women. Raising the value of such work also raises the value of work that women normally do, and thus raises the status of women. At the point of a divorce, the woman will find that a court can order that she receive a just and equitable share of the matrimonial assets. Her homemaking and childcaring has earned her some proportionate ownership of the couple's matrimonial assets. Her contribution towards the family is recognized by the law and the court is able to give a practical expression of such recognition.

Affirms the moral view of marriage

When a Family Court makes an order that two former marital partners should each receive a just and equitable share of the matrimonial assets, this affirms that their marriage has been their equal cooperative partnership of different efforts. The husband and wife have been making different kinds of contributions towards their marital partnership. The law does not differentiate between the various kinds. Upon the termination of their partnership by divorce, it follows that each party should get a just and equitable share. It is each party's entitlement. He or she has earned this just and equitable share of the matrimonial assets whether by his or her going out to make money, or staying home to take care of the home, family and children.

Moral message at divorce

Even though divorce is somewhat unfortunate as it means the termination of a marriage, the law can continue to expound a moral message to the divorced parties. It is a good law that aims to expound a moral message to a husband and wife both during the subsistence of their marriage and even on its termination by divorce.

IX MUSLIMS

49. To what extent does the Women's Charter apply to Muslim Singaporeans?

General statute

Only from a layman's point of view is the Women's Charter a non-Muslim family statute. It is in fact one among the general statutes of the Republic of Singapore. Section 3(1) provides that the Women's Charter applies to all persons in Singapore. The only qualification comes within section 3(2) which provides that some parts of it do not apply to persons who are married under Muslim law. Those exclusions from application, however, still leave many parts of the Women's Charter applicable even to persons who are married under Muslim law.

Formation of a non-Muslim marriage

The part of the Women's Charter regulating the formation of non-Muslim marriage (discussed in Part II above) are clearly not applicable to persons who are married under Muslim law. These provisions were enacted to replace the separate marriage laws that existed previously which applied only to non-Muslim Singaporeans according to the ethnic group they belong to or their religious affiliation.

Termination of a non-Muslim marriage

The parts of the Women's Charter on termination of a non-Muslim marriage by divorce (discussed in Part VI above) are also not applicable to persons married under Muslim law.

Regulation of spouses in a non-Muslim marriage

The parts of the Women's Charter regulating a husband-wife relationship within a non-Muslim marriage (discussed in Part III above) are also not applicable to persons married under Muslim law.

Protection from violence within the family

The parts of the Women's Charter on protection from violence within the family (discussed in Part V above) do apply to all Singaporeans whether married or unmarried and, if married, whether under non-Muslim or Muslim law. The infliction or threat of violence is unacceptable whatever the religion of the parties and, if married, whether under non-Muslim or Muslim law.

Regulation of the relationship between parent and child

The parts of the Women's Charter regulating the relationship between parents and their child (discussed in Part IV above) do apply to all Singaporeans, irrespective of whether the parents are non-Muslim or Muslim, and, if the parents are married, whether under non-Muslim law or Muslim law. While the particular religion of the parents may be a factor for consideration by a court when reviewing an application before it, the law does not change according to the parents' religion.

Maintenance

The parts of the Women's Charter regulating the provision

of maintenance to a child (discussed in Part VII above) apply to all Singaporeans.

So do the parts of the Women's Charter on maintenance of a wife during the subsistence of her marriage (also discussed in Part VII above). A wife married under Muslim law may use these parts of the Women's Charter. It should be noted that there are also rules within Muslim law regarding the maintenance of a wife. The existence of two sets of rules available to a woman married under Muslim law means that a Muslim wife can avail herself of either the law of maintenance of a wife by her husband under the Women's Charter, or the equivalent under Muslim law.

50. To what extent can a Muslim Singaporean choose to have the parts of the Women's Charter that would generally not be applicable to him or her become applicable?

There is a degree of choice available to a Muslim Singaporean.

One Muslim can marry a non-Muslim under the Women's Charter

Even of marriage itself, the Women's Charter has provided since 1967 that a Muslim person can choose to marry a non-Muslim person under the non-Muslim marriage law contained in the Women's Charter. Where such a marriage is solemnized, the non-Muslim married person will subsequently be fully regulated by provisions in the Women's Charter in matters relating to his or her marriage.

Maintenance of a divorced wife, custody of child, and division of matrimonial assets

The parts of the Women's Charter on maintenance of a divorced wife, custody of a child, and division of matrimonial assets are inherently tied to the termination of a non-Muslim marriage by a judgement of divorce granted by the Family Court. As a result of this, these parts are excluded from application to a person who was party to a Muslim marriage that has since been terminated by divorce. The party to a Muslim marriage should look to Muslim law for equivalent applications rather than these parts of the Women's Charter.

By a statutory amendment in 1999, however, the Singapore Parliament has allowed Muslim parties to choose to apply under these parts of the Women's Charter instead of under Muslim law. Upon the termination of a Muslim marriage which termination has been recorded by the Muslim Syariah Court, the two divorced Muslim parties can by their agreement choose to make an application for any or all of these matters to the Family Court. On such an application by Muslim divorced parties, the Family Court will proceed to hear their applications and resolve them using the law in the Women's Charter.

By this change, then, a Muslim person has greater choice than previously as he or she has the option now to be regulated by the non-Muslim law in the Women's Charter. It is conceivable that one day all Singaporeans, whether Muslim or non-Muslim, may be regulated by one unified law that takes appropriate consideration of the effect of religious differences. In Question 8 above it was said that the Women's Charter already allows religious rites during the process of solemnizing a marriage. There is no reason to think that similar allowances cannot be as easily made, where appropriate, in other areas of family law to cater to various religious affiliations.

Such a unified family law does not as yet exist today. When it does, Singaporeans might well take pride in a family law that is one more institution uniting Singaporeans of various ethnic backgrounds and religious affiliations.

EPILOGUE

EPILOGUE

As this book was going to press the government announced its proposal to amend some provisions in the Women's Charter. If these changes become law, there are several amendments or additional points I would like to make to some of my answers in this book. For the moment it is not known if they will become law or what final form the changes will assume. For reference, I suggest here how I would alter parts of seven of my answers if the changes became law.

6. What are the formalities of marriage in Singapore?

It is proposed to maintain the requirement of 15-day residence in Singapore before the issuance of a marriage licence only where "any party to the intended marriage is not a citizen or permanent resident of Singapore".

It is also proposed that specific groups of persons be identified by subsidiary legislation (possibly persons under a particular age or persons who have previously become divorced) who will be required to attend marriage preparation courses before the marriage licence they seek is issued to them.

It is also proposed that, where one of the parties seeking a marriage licence was previously divorced, he or she should declare, as one item of the statutory declaration, whether he or she has any maintenance arrears owing towards a child or children from the previous marriage or towards a former wife.

9. How does the law of marriage apply to foreigners who wish to marry in Singapore?

It is proposed that the requirement of 15-day residence in Singapore applies only where both parties are not Singapore citizens or permanent residents.

33. What community assistance — legal and non-legal — is available to a couple going through a divorce?

It is proposed that, where the divorce proceedings involves a child who is below 21 years old or children below this age, the couple must attend compulsory counselling and mediation on areas of disagreement relating to the child or children.

It is also proposed to empower the Family Court to make further orders as deemed appropriate where the parties fail to attend counselling as directed by the Court. These may take the form of an order to hold the divorce proceedings in abeyance or that the uncooperative party should pay the costs of the proceedings.

36. How is the duty of a parent to maintain a child related with parental responsibility?

It is proposed to further make clear that a parent's duty to maintain his or her child continues despite the termination of the parents' marriage. This is achieved by extending the power of the Family Court to make orders of financial provision even where the judgement of divorce had been obtained outside Singapore.

37. Who, between a husband and wife, has the duty to provide reasonable maintenance to the other?

It is proposed to extend the power of the Family Court to order financial provision, including that the former husband should continue to provide reasonable maintenance to his former wife, even where the judgement of divorce was obtained outside Singapore.

39. How is an order of maintenance enforced?

It is proposed to enhance enforcement to better secure the timely payment of maintenance that had been ordered by the Family Court. The Court shall be empowered to order a defaulter to post a banker's guarantee against future defaults, to undergo financial counselling and also to impose a 40-hour community service order on the defaulter. Compliance with these does not excuse the payment of the sum that was owed. Further, the claimants of the maintenance order may report the maintenance debt to relevant credit bureaus.

It is also proposed that it should be possible for a claimant to obtain the defaulter's employment information from the CPF Board, that the Family Court should be empowered to order the parties to provide information on their financial status in maintenance proceedings and for power to provide for service of summons in connection with an application for maintenance to be done by registered post.

41. What does the Women's Charter allow of the matrimonial assets of a couple upon their divorce?

It is proposed to extend the power of the Family Court to order the just and equitable division of matrimonial assets between the spouses upon their divorce even where the judgement of divorce had been obtained outside of Singapore.

It is also proposed that, upon receipt of his or her share of these matrimonial assets, the divorced parent may be ordered to deposit some of this property's worth into the Children's Development Account of a child or children to whom the parent continues to be financially responsible.

REFERENCES

If you wish to read further on this subject, please refer to the following selected writings on the family law in Singapore.

General
Leong, Wai Kum. *Elements of Family Law in Singapore*. Singapore: LexisNexis, 2007.

Part I
Leong, Wai Kum. "Fifty Years and More of the Women's Charter". *Singapore Journal of Legal Studies* (2008): 1–24.

Part II
Leong, Wai Kum. "Clarity in the Law of Valid, Void and Voidable Non-Muslim Marriages". *Singapore Academy of Law Journal* 21 (2009): 575–90.
———. "Transsexual in England Still of Birth Sex Even If This Transgresses European Human Rights Convention: *Bellinger v Bellinger*". *Singapore Journal of Legal Studies* (2003): 274–84.
———. "Formation of Marriage in England and Singapore by Contract: Void Marriage and Non-marriage". *International Journal of Law, Policy and the Family* 14 (2000): 256–80.
———. "A Fresh Look at Void Marriage: *Gereis v Yagoub*". *Singapore Journal of Legal Studies* (1997): 580–84.
———. "Solemnization of Marriage: Conceptualisation and Statutory Interpretation". *Singapore Journal of Legal Studies* (1995): 283–314.
———. "Reform of the Law of Nullity in the Women's Charter". *Singapore Journal of Legal Studies* (1992): 1–21.
Ong, Siew Ling, Debbie. "The Test of Sex for Marriage in Singapore". *International Journal of Law, Policy and the Family* 12 (1998): 161–79.

————. "Local Developments on Foreign Marriages and Divorce: *Ho Ah Chye v Hsinchieh Hsu Irene, Asha Maudgil v Suresh Kumar Gosain*". *Singapore Academy of Law Journal* (1994).

Tan, Carol. " 'We Are Registered': Actual Processes and the Law of Marriage in Singapore". *International Journal of Law, Policy and the Family* 12 (1999): 1–32.

Part III

Leong, Wai Kum. "Prenuptial Agreement on Division of Matrimonial Assets Subject to Court Scrutiny". *Singapore Journal of Legal Studies* (2009): 211–25.

————. "Supporting Marriage Through Description as an Equal Partnership of Efforts". In *International Survey of Family Law*, edited by Andrew Bainham. UK: Jordans, 2002.

Ong, Siew Ling, Debbie. "Prenuptial Agreements: A Singaporean Perspective in *TQ v TR*". *Children and Family Law Quarterly* 21 (2009): 536–47.

————. "Prenuptial Agreements and Foreign Matrimonial Agreements: *TQ v TR*". *Singapore Academy of Law Journal* (2007): 397–408.

————. "When Spouses Agree". *Singapore Academy of Law Journal* 18 (2006): 96–115.

Part IV

Chan, Wing Cheong. "Custody Orders, Parental Responsibility and Academic Contributions". *Singapore Journal of Legal Studies* (2005): 407–15.

————. "The Law in Singapore on Child Abduction". *Singapore Journal of Legal Studies* (2004): 444–61.

————. "Applications under the Guardianship of Infants Act". *Singapore Journal of Legal Studies* (1998): 182–90.

————. "Changes to the Juvenile Justice System". *Singapore Journal of Legal Studies* (1994): 448–56.

Leong, Wai Kum. "Legal Implications of Paternity Testing". In *Life Sciences: Law and Ethics*, edited by Kaan T. and Liu E.T. Singapore: Singapore Academy of Law and Bioethics Advisory Committee, 2006.

————. "A Communitarian Effort in Guardianship and Custody of Children after Parents' Divorce". In *The International Survey of Family Law*, edited by Andrew Bainham. UK: Jordans, 2006.

————. "The Convention on the Civil Aspects of International Child Abduction — A Case for Singapore to be a Member State". *Singapore Law Gazette* (2005): 19–26.

————. "Restatement of the Law of Guardianship and Custody in Singapore". *Singapore Journal of Legal Studies* (1999): 432–93.

————. "International Co-operation in Child Abduction Across Borders". *Singapore Academy of Law Journal* (1999): 409–33.

————. "Trends and Developments in Family Law". In *Review of the Judicial and Legal Reforms in Singapore between 1990 and 1995*, edited by Walter Woon. Singapore: Singapore Academy of Law, 1996.

Lowe, Nigel and Debbie Ong. "Why The Child Abduction Protocol Negotiations Should Not Deflect Singapore From Acceding To The 1980 Hague Abduction Convention". *Singapore Journal of Legal Studies* 2 (2007): 216–39.

Ong, Siew Ling, Debbie. "Parental Relocation Across Borders: Is Relocation in the Child's Welfare?" *The Singapore Law Gazette* (July 2009): 34–37.

————. "Parental Child Abduction in Singapore: The Experience of a Non-Convention Country". *International Journal of Law, Policy and the Family* 21 (2007): 220–41.

———. "The Next Step In Post-Divorce Parenting". *Singapore Academy of Law Journal* 17 (2005): 648–67.

———. "Making No Custody Order". *Singapore Journal of Legal Studies* (2003): 583–92.

———. "Proof of Paternity and Access to Non-Biological Child: *Re A (An Infant)*". *Singapore Academy of Law Journal* 15 (2003): 399–408.

———. "Parents and Custody Orders — A New Approach". *Singapore Journal of Legal Studies* (1999): 205–28.

Ong, Debbie and Stella Quah. "Grandparenting in Divorced Families". *Singapore Journal of Legal Studies* (2007): 25–50.

Wee, Kenneth. "The Law of Legitimacy in Singapore". *Malaya Law Review* 18 (1976): 1–25.

Part VI

Chan, Wing Cheong. "The Court's Powers Under the Women's Charter When the Respondent Opposes Divorce Petition". *Singapore Journal of Legal Studies* (1999): 573–95.

———. "Trends in Non-Muslim Divorces in Singapore". *International Journal of Law, Policy and the Family* 22 (2008): 91–121.

Leong, Wai Kum. "A Turning Point in Singapore Family Law". *Malaya Law Review* 21 (1979): 327–51.

Ong, Siew Ling, Debbie. "Time Restriction on Divorce in Singapore". *Singapore Journal of Legal Studies* (2003): 418–43.

———. "The Singapore Family Court: Family Law in Practice". *International Journal of Law, Policy and the Family* 13 (1999): 328–49.

Part VII

Chan, Wing Cheong. "The Duty to Support an Aged Parent in

Singapore". *Pacific Rim Law and Policy Journal* 13 (2004): 547–78.

Leong, Wai Kum. Private Representation *Report of the Select Committee of Parliament on the Women's Charter (Amendment) Bill [Bill No. 5/96]*, B22–B39. Singapore: Government Printers, 1996.

———. Private Representation *Report of the Select Committee of Parliament on the Women's Charter (Amendment) Bill 1979*, A1–A15. Singapore: Government Printers, 1980.

———. "The Duty to Maintain Spouse and Children During Marriage". *Malaya Law Review* 29 (1987): 56–79.

Part VIII

Crown, Barry. "Property Division on Dissolution of Marriage". *Malaya Law Review* 30 (1988): 34–61.

Leong, Wai Kum. "Division of Matrimonial Assets Upon Divorce — Lessons from Singapore for Malaysian Practice". In *Developments in Singapore and Malaysian Law*, edited by Alan Tan and Azmi Sharom. Singapore: Marshall Cavendish, 2007.

———. "Division of Matrimonial Assets: Order in the Fairest Possible Way". In *International Survey of Family Law*, edited by Andrew Bainham. UK: Jordans, 2004.

———. "The Laws in Singapore and England Affecting Spouses' Property on Divorce". *Singapore Journal of Legal Studies* (2001): 19–52.

———. "The Just and Equitable Division of Gains Between Equal Partners in Marriage". *Singapore Journal of Legal Studies* (2000): 208–40.

———. "Division of Matrimonial Assets: Recent Cases and Thoughts for Reform". *Singapore Journal of Legal Studies* (1993): 351–400.

———. "Division of Matrimonial Property Upon Termination of Marriage". *Malayan Law Journal* 1 (1989): xiii–xviii.

Ong, Debbie. "HDB Policies: Shaping Family Practice". *Singapore Journal of Legal Studies* (2000): 110–19.

INDEX

ABOUT THE AUTHOR

Leong Wai Kum is Professor at the Faculty of Law, National
University of Singapore.

www.ingramcontent.com/pod-product-compliance
Lightning Source LLC
Chambersburg PA
CBHW021536260326
41914CB00001B/32